RAND

A Method for Measuring the Value of Scout/ Reconnaissance

Clairice T. Veit, Monti D. Callero

Arroyo Center

The research described in this report was sponsored by the United States Army under Contract MDA903-91-C-0006.

Library of Congress Cataloging in Publication Data

Veit, Clairice T.
   A method for measuring the value of scout/reconnaissance   /
Clairice T. Veit, Monti D. Callero.
      p.   cm
   "Prepared for the United States Army."
   "Arroyo Center."
   MR-476-A
   ISBN 0-8330-1639-3 (alk.paper)
   1. Scouts and scouting—Computer simulation.   2. Military
reconnaissance—Computer simulation.   I. Callero, Monti D.
II. United States.   Army.   III. Title.
U220.V45   1995
355.4´13—dc20   95-8314
                                                                  CIP

RAND
Copyright © 1995

RAND is a nonprofit institution that helps improve public policy through research and analysis. RAND's publications do not necessarily reflect the opinions or policies of its research sponsors.

Published 1995 by RAND
1700 Main Street, P.O. Box 2138, Santa Monica, CA 90407-2138
RAND URL: http://www.rand.org/
To order RAND documents or to obtain additional information, contact Distribution
Services: Telephone: (310) 451-7002; Fax: (310) 451-6915; Internet: order@rand.org/

RAND

A Method for Measuring the Value of Scout/ Reconnaissance

Clairice T. Veit, Monti D. Callero

Prepared for the
United States Army

Arroyo Center

Preface

This report describes a method for quantitatively analyzing scout and reconnaissance systems in a way that accounts for both technological considerations and human performance in an operational context. The method is system independent; it can be applied to measuring the value of any type of system conducting scout/recon and is relevant to any ground-combat force, organization, or composition. The method fills a critical gap in analytical support for scout/recon system development and acquisition decisionmaking by providing an analytical basis for measuring and comparing combat intelligence systems in terms of resulting operational performance. It uses carefully developed expert-judgment models of the human processes of situation assessment and operational decisionmaking; it uses high-resolution operator-interactive simulation of scout/recon system operations to represent a system's performance on the battlefield.

This research was done for the project on Combat Aviation Issues, sponsored by the Director of Force Development, Deputy Chief of Staff for Operations, and was conducted in the Arroyo Center's Force Development and Technology Program. The Arroyo Center is a federally funded research and development center sponsored by the United States Army.

Contents

Figures

Tables

Summary

A longstanding problem for those making decisions about scout/reconnaissance (scout/recon) systems development and acquisition has been the lack of analytical tools with which to quantify, and hence comparatively evaluate, the operational value of scout/recon systems, concepts, and technologies. The greatest difficulty in conducting quantitative analysis of scout/recon systems is the modeling of human assessment and decisionmaking processes that link scout/recon inputs to operational results. The essence of a scout/recon system's value is not the intelligence items it produces per se, but how well it supports the situation assessment and operational decisionmaking processes that influence battle outcomes.

This report describes the development and use of a method for conducting quantitative analysis of scout/recon systems that can account for the operational and technological aspects of a system's mission, and also for the system's effects on the assessment and decisionmaking processes. The method is system independent; it can be applied to measuring the value of any type of system conducting scout/recon. It provides an analytical basis to support development and acquisition decisionmaking in terms of resulting operational performance.

We used different research approaches to address the different elements of technology, military doctrine and concepts, and human information processing that all play a role in how scout/recon capabilities affect battle outcomes. We modeled the human processes by applying psychological measurement techniques to the judgments of experts who perform those processes. We applied high-resolution, operator-interactive computer models to simulate scout/recon missions in representative combat environments to determine a system's performance. In the scout/recon analysis method, these simulation results and other information describing a particular scout/recon system and operating environment are input to the human-process model that calculates their effects on operational performance. The analysis method provides the capability to compare different scout/recon systems, extant or proposed, and to highlight scout/recon characteristics that provide high payoff potential.

The Backdrop

We set our research against a backdrop of heavy (armored and mechanized infantry) division operations, because the division plays a central role in the conduct of battle and in the development and use of intelligence. We consider two division operations: a prepared defense against an enemy attack and a deliberate attack against a prepared enemy defense. The time period is the critical 36 hours prior to initial contact between the lead combat elements, during which the division seeks to clarify the enemy's operational plan and intention, locate key enemy units and their movement patterns, and make final adjustments to division forces so as to have the best chance of winning the battle.

Below we describe the human-process model and its development. We then describe how we used our simulations to determine the performance capabilities of different scout/recon systems, and how the human-process and simulation models provide an analytic method to compare capabilities from different scout/recon systems with respect to their effects on operational outcomes.

The Human-Process Model

The Human Processes

A major research objective was to explain the human processes that link scout/recon information to operational performance. We broke these processes into three areas:

- *Collection Management.* Planning the division's organic intelligence collection requirements, monitoring source and content of intelligence data, dynamically identifying additional needs, and reacting to special intelligence requests to support the situation assessment process that arise as the conflict situation develops.

- *Situation Assessment.* Scrutinizing intelligence inputs from all sources, including the division's organic scout/recon assets, to determine all things possible to know about the enemy that would assist the division in preparing for combat, particularly to identify and track key enemy force elements.

- *Operational Performance.* The combat performance of the forces as a result of the decisionmaking process that follows from the situation assessment input and other factors pertaining to the operational situation.

The Model

We applied the subjective transfer function (STF) method (Veit and Callero, 1982; Veit, Callero, and Rose, 1984) to develop a scout/recon measurement model (SCRMM) of these three processes. The SCRMM is depicted by the structure shown in Figure S.1.

Figure S.1 identifies the factors associated with each of the human processes outlined above, Collection Management (lowest tier), Situation Assessment (middle tier), and Operational Performance (top tier) that link to the overall model outcome, Percent of Key Force Elements That Could Be Defeated. Each hierarchy in Figure S.1 links to the adjacent hierarchical tier through its measure of performance (MOP); each textured square represents the MOP for the set of factors shown below it. It is this MOP-linking feature that characterizes an STF structure. Later we discuss the details of how we developed the SCRMM's STF structure shown in Figure S.1.

The measurement feature of the SCRMM stems from the STF method's use of modern psychological measurement techniques (e.g., Anderson, 1970, 1981; Birnbaum, 1974; Birnbaum and Veit, 1974a, 1974b; Birnbaum, 1978, 1980; Krantz et al., 1971; Krantz and Tversky, 1971; Veit, 1978). The basic concept of modern subjective measurement is to construct experimental designs to *test* hypotheses about how people value and process information contained in situations to which they respond. Hypotheses are theories of the judgment data expressed in the form of algebraic functions. Experimental designs must allow distinction among different theories' predictions; thus, when a theory passes its tests, it has received empirical support for its validity as a representation of how people value and process information. The resulting algebraic subjective measurement functions mathematically link the hierarchies via the MOPs to form the SCRMM.

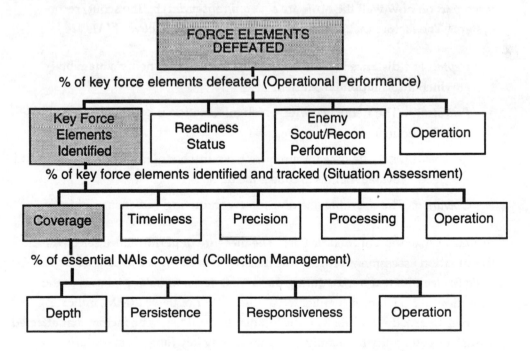

Figure S.1—Scout/Recon Measurement Model (SCRMM)

These functions are referred to as subjective transfer functions (STFs) because functions lower in the hierarchy *transfer* their outputs for use in the function at the next-higher level in the hierarchy.

Each of the hierarchical tiers shown in Figure S.1 contains the factors used to construct situations for subject matter experts (SMEs) to judge in terms of their effects on the associated MOP. The algebraic measurement theories that explained those judgments are discussed later. The factors defining each of the hierarchical levels are presented next.

Collection Management (lowest tier). The measure of performance for the collection management process is the *percent of essential named areas of interest (NAIs) that could be covered in a timely manner.* This MOP is highlighted as the factor Coverage at the second tier in the model because it is also a factor that *affects* the situation assessment process. Thus, this factor, Coverage, serves to link the collection management and situation assessment processes in the SCRMM.

The idea behind NAIs is as follows: During the intelligence preparation of the battlefield, division intelligence officers designate NAIs in locations on the battlefield that are important places to monitor enemy activity (e.g., bridges, road divisions). As a battle unfolds, other areas might become important. The ability of the situation assessment staff to provide operations officers and the commander with a complete picture of the enemy's force posture depends in large part on how well the NAIs are covered (observed) by the scout/recon system. The factors that affected SMEs' judged ability to cover NAIs are

- *Depth.* The distance behind the forward trace of the enemy's main body at which information is collected.

- *Persistence.* The frequency with which information is collected at each NAI (revisit frequency).

- *Responsiveness.* The time from requesting nonscheduled reconnaissance until a collection system begins to collect the data.

- *Operation.* The operation the division is conducting—offense or defense.

Situation Assessment (middle tier). The measure of performance selected for the situation assessment process was the *percent of enemy key force elements that could be identified and tracked* during the critical decisionmaking phases of the operation. This factor is highlighted at the top tier of the SCRMM, indicating that it serves to link the middle with the top hierarchical tier. The factors that affected SMEs' judged ability to identify and track enemy key force elements are

- *Coverage.* The percent of the NAIs that were covered.

- *Timeliness.* Time between information collection and its availability for use by the situation assessor.

- *Precision.* The level of detail about enemy weapon systems reported by the scout/recon system—detection, classification (distinction between tracked and wheeled vehicles), or recognition (distinction of type of tracked or wheeled vehicles).

- *Processing.* How information is interpreted and displayed—manual, semiautomated, or fully automated.

- *Operation.* The operation the division is conducting—offense or defense.

Operational Performance (highest tier). The overall measure of performance shown at the top of the structure as the final MOP is the *percent of enemy units that could be defeated.* Factors that affected this MOP are

- *Percent of Key Force Elements That Were Identified and Tracked.*

- *Readiness Status of Division Forces.* The division's percent readiness scale as determined by standard Army readiness status ratings. In the context of imminent combat addressed here, readiness status is the proportion of maximum potential combat power that the division can achieve based on authorized equipment that is serviceable, personnel that are trained, and support capability required to sustain the battle; it reflects the operational readiness of each subordinate combat unit accumulated across the division.

- *Enemy's Scout/Recon Performance.* The distance behind friendly lines at which the enemy was able to perform scout/recon as a result of the enemy's capability and the division's counterrecon ability.

- *Operation.* The operation the division is conducting—offense or defense.

Developing the SCRMM

Constructing an STF Hierarchical Structure

Constructing an STF structure requires a thorough understanding of the processes being modeled in terms of the factors that affect them and the MOPs that reflect their outputs. To that end, researchers participate in in-depth discussions with SMEs and, when possible, observe them performing their activities. Interactions with SMEs aid the researcher in selecting, defining, and hierarchically organizing judgment factors and MOPs so that three criteria are met: (1) judgment tasks defined by the factors and MOPs are meaningful to

SMEs with regard to their activities and objectives, (2) judgment experiments can be performed at each hierarchical level using modern measurement techniques to determine SMEs' subjective measurement theory, and (3) judgment tasks are hierarchically structured (in this case to reflect the sequential activities of collection management, situation assessment, and operational performance) so that measurement theories that pass their tests can mathematically link the hierarchical levels.

In the scout/recon study, the directors of intelligence (G-2) and of operations (G-3) from the 4th Infantry Division (Mechanized), 1st Cavalry Division (Armored), 1st Armor Division, and 3rd Infantry Division (Mechanized) selected their best-qualified officers to participate in our study. Between 10 and 13 officers from each area—collection management, situation assessment, and operations—participated in discussions about the details of their activities. These discussions and observations of SMEs' performance in command-post exercises produced the set of factors and MOPs that satisfied the above-stated criteria for the STF structure shown in Figure S.1.

Designing Experiments and Analyzing Judgment Data in the Modern Measurement Framework

The subjective measurement theories for each hierarchical level shown in Figure S.1 (referred to as STFs once a theory is determined for each level and they are functionally interlinked) were obtained in the modern subjective measurement framework described briefly earlier. The basic measurement idea is to formulate experimental designs that allow validity testing of algebraic measurement theories that potentially could explain the experts' judgments. If a proposed theory fails tests imposed on it by the experimental design, it is rejected as wrong. When a theory passes its tests, it and its parameter values (estimated from the data) are accepted as the appropriate measurement function (STF) in the STF hierarchical model.

Experimental designs. The factorial combination of factors—that is, the procedure of crossing each level of each factor with each level of every other factor (factor levels used in the experiments are presented in the body of the report)—is a prominent experimental design feature for testing among competing algebraic theories. However, this design feature alone is not sufficient for testing among some theories (e.g., adding versus averaging) that might be reasonable competitors. For our judgment experiments we used full factorial designs that included all factor combinations, as well as smaller factorial design subsets, thus making it possible to distinguish among a number of different theories.

Data collection procedures. SMEs met in groups of from three to six. Sessions began with a viewgraph briefing and hourlong discussion of the combat backdrop, the factors, factor levels, MOP, and representative situations described in the questionnaire; then the SMEs filled out their individual questionnaires. The purpose of the rather lengthy and detailed discussion was for SMEs to establish a familiarity with the task (especially for those who had not previously participated in factor-selection sessions) and the questionnaire format, and to set a common context for all participants in which to make their judgments.

Data analyses. Seventy-five SMEs participated in the judgment experiments. Analysis of the judgment data for each SME group—collection management, situation assessment, and operational performance—revealed interactions among the factors in their effects on judged MOPs, thus ruling out all theories that predict independence among factors (e.g., additive and averaging theories). A multiplicative theory and a configural-weight theory were tested to account for these interactions but were rejected when we found systematic deviations from their predictions. The geometric averaging theory accounted for these systematic deviations and provided a good explanation of all three sets of judgment data. We present tests of this theory for the three sets of data in the body of the report.

Scout/Reconnaissance Mission Simulation

A major feature of the scout/recon analysis method is to determine a scout/recon system's performance by simulating scout/recon missions. We did this using high-resolution, operator-interactive combat models that were capable of representing the important characteristics of scout/recon systems and the operational environment. These simulations directly determine two factors for input to the SCRMM: the **depth** a system could penetrate behind the enemy's forward trace to gather intelligence information, and the level of **precision** (detection, classification, or recognition) of that information. Additionally, during these simulation runs, scout/recon tactics, techniques, and procedures can be assessed with respect to mission accomplishment and system survivability. A system's survival is critical to mission accomplishment not only in the sense that a system that has an unacceptably low survival rate is not a viable candidate, but also in the sense that the tactics that must be used *in order to survive* can have a dominant effect on its depth of coverage behind the enemy's forward trace and on the precision level of the information it can obtain. Thus, a scout/recon system's survivability is reflected in its depth and precision capabilities.

For our research, we used the suite of high-resolution, interfaced combat models in RAND's Combat Analysis Environment (CAE) that provide the capability for operators to interactively conduct scout/recon missions against maneuvering enemy forces. The CAE models are designed to incorporate and apply detailed representations of a scout/recon system's characteristics so that the operator conducts the missions within the capabilities and limitations afforded by the particular system being investigated. The CAE models allow sensor representations of multiple, independently selectable and controllable sensors (e.g., FLIR, TV, radar, eyeball), operator specification of fields-of-view that present corresponding ranges for detection, classification, and recognition under specified atmospheric and clutter conditions, and automatic scan capability. Other representations include aircraft survivability technology, radar cross section and thermal emission signatures, and physical dimensions of the systems. Detailed flight dynamics data are incorporated to accurately determine flight maneuvers called for by the pilots to assure that simulated aerial profiles do not exceed the flight limitations of the simulated aircraft.

As an exploratory example, we used the CAE to construct scenarios in rolling terrain and in hilly, forested terrain. Army intelligence officers identified NAIs for those scenarios. Army pilots flew simulated scout/recon missions in a representation of an advanced scout/recon helicopter. Although the helicopter characteristics were represented in detail, the pilots alone were responsible for flying in a manner consistent with the tactical environment with respect to speed, obstacle clearance, and altitude above the surface. Their responsibility also included allowing sufficient time for manual or automatic sensor operation during mission maneuvers, e.g., remaining unmasked long enough to complete the sensor tasks. During the mission, the pilots reacted to what they saw visually or with sensors and to what their survival equipment (e.g., radar warning) indicated; they employed scout/recon tactics and doctrine applicable to the scout/recon aircraft and their perceived threat situation. By analyzing these missions in detail, the precision of the information obtained about enemy systems and the depth of penetration could be determined.

The pilots who participated in the missions adapted readily to the CAE's mission and flight procedures and to its simulation artificialities and were satisfied that the mission results were credible.

Applying the Method

The SCRMM can be used for analysis either within the framework of the overall method to measure the value of a specified scout/recon system(s) or as a stand-alone analysis tool to explore and assess notional systems or concepts and seek to identify system enhancements or tradeoffs with high marginal payoffs.

Analytic Measures

The SCRMM's highest measurement factor, the one that indicates contribution to a heavy division's operational effectiveness, is **key force elements defeated** (the percent of key enemy force elements that the division could defeat). Additional measures of interest pertaining to the performance of the intelligence gathering and assessment processes are **key force elements identified** (the percent of key enemy force elements that could be identified and tracked) and **coverage** (the percent of essential NAIs that could be covered in a timely manner). The latter two measures provide a means to identify and assess preferred initiatives to improve the division's intelligence capability as an independent endeavor, to include enhancements to the scout/recon systems, communications systems and procedures, and internal information processing capability. The higher-level operational effectiveness measure then provides the means to consider improvements in relation to how they affect the division's overall fighting ability and compare intelligence enhancements with other approaches to achieving similar improvements, such as greater emphasis on counterreconnaissance or maintaining higher states of division readiness.

Because of its general usage, commonality, and historical significance in assessing a division's fighting potential, operational readiness provides an important comparison alternative for analyzing relative contributions of different scout/recon or other division intelligence systems. The concept is to determine what change in readiness level would be required (in the judgments of the SMEs modeled by the SCRMM) to achieve the same difference in percent of key enemy force elements defeated that resulted from different scout/recon or intelligence system capabilities. This change in readiness provides a useful measure to compare the different systems' contributions to heavy division combat capability. We call this concept **readiness substitution**.

Analyzing a Specified Scout/Recon System(s)

The steps in applying the method to analyze a specified scout/recon system are (1) determine the scout/recon system's depth and precision levels by using simulation techniques such as those described above, (2) determine factor levels for each of the other factors contained in the SCRMM, (3) use the SCRMM to compute the MOPs, and (4) use the MOPs to evaluate the scout/recon system in the context of the circumstances defined by the factor levels.

Factor levels must be determined for each factor in the hierarchical model in order to compute the SCRMM. Precision and Depth are determined from conducting scout/recon missions in a simulation scenario(s) as described above. Factor levels for Readiness Status, Processing, and Operation come directly from the military situations and scenarios of interest to an analysis. Persistence and Responsiveness are affected by scout/recon resource constraints, how scout/recon resources would be allocated between these two activities and, for aircraft systems, the ability of the aviation unit to generate flights. The Timeliness of information available to assess the enemy's situation depends both on the technique used by the scout/recon system to communicate its findings back to the division and the means by which its information is processed once it arrives. Enemy Scout/Recon Performance, the ability of their systems to find and maintain surveillance on friendly forces, reflects both the enemy's capabilities and the division's counterreconnaissance operations.

Once the factor levels are determined, the MOP factors—Coverage, Key Force Elements-Identified, and Key Force Elements Defeated—are computed by the SCRMM. For comparisons among multiple scout/recon systems, the MOPs for each system and the resulting readiness substitution measures provide the operational effectiveness inputs for integration into the overall decision process.

To assure understanding of this focal application of the scout/recon analysis method, we provide a comprehensive example to conclude the report.

Stand-Alone Use of the SCRMM

The SCRMM was automated to produce an easy-to-use program for assessing the effects of different scout/recon and intelligence system capabilities by allowing a user to modify or select factor levels throughout the structure to define systems and conditions of interest and evaluate resulting differences in MOPs. This use of the SCRMM could provide valuable information to development and acquisition decisions beyond that provided for a specific system(s) under consideration.

One important application is to perform sensitivity analyses (i.e., how sensitive the MOPs are to changes in the factor levels) on the results obtained from analyzing a specified scout/recon system(s). In this context, investigating the effects of varying non-mission-dependent factors (i.e., all except depth and precision) can be accomplished simply by changing the relevant factor level(s) in the SCRMM and recomputing. Sensitivities of the MOPs to depth and precision variation can be *directly* assessed in the same way; however, investigating sensitivities to scout/recon *system characteristics* that affect its depth and precision factor levels (e.g., sensor representations, signature estimates) would likely require that the mission simulations be reconducted.

Another important application is to explore and assess notional systems or concepts, determine factor level requirement options that would achieve a selected MOP value (e.g., 75% key force elements identified), or to identify system enhancements or tradeoffs that yield high marginal payoffs. To assess loosely defined notional systems or concepts, a controlled sequence of SCRMM runs would be made that included factor levels spanning the uncertainties of the systems' capability. Determining options to achieve selected MOP values would be done by systematically varying factor levels over a sequence of SCRMM runs. Identifying areas of high marginal payoff would follow from graphical analysis of SCRMM results.

Graphical Tradeoff Analyses

Numerous tradeoffs among factors that can be calculated by the SCRMM program can also be viewed graphically in the report. An example is provided in Figure S.2, where the geometric averaging theory's predictions of percent of key enemy force elements identified and tracked are plotted on the y-axis as a function of the percent of NAIs covered by the collection management cell on the x-axis; a separate curve is for each level of information precision: detection, classification, or recognition. The situations shown in Figure S.2 are as follows: friendlies are in a prepared defense, intelligence information is processed manually by the situation assessment cell and is available for use five minutes after being observed by a scout/recon system.

Tradeoffs are highlighted by the vertical and horizontal lines. For systems that can provide detection information with a 25% NAI coverage level, a direct high marginal payoff in the key force elements identified MOP can be attained from sensor enhancements that would permit classification or recognition (increasing the MOP from 18% at the detection level to 26% (classification level) to 35% (recognition level), respectively). In fact, improving the precision level to classification would provide the same payoff as would increasing coverage to 47% while maintaining the precision level at detection; a recognition precision level at 25% NAI coverage is equivalent to 70% coverage with detection. Note

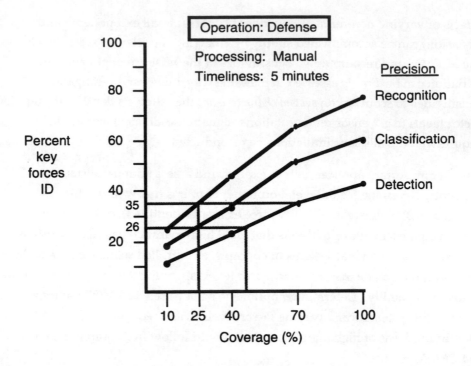

Figure S.2—Graphical Tradeoff Assessment

also, from both horizontal lines we see that recognition has high marginal payoff over classification. For example, the same MOP value is attainable by 10% coverage with recognition that can be attained by 25% coverage with classification. These observations suggest that sensor enhancements provide a high potential for improving scout/recon effectiveness or maintaining its effectiveness at less risk and exposure to enemy air defenses. Other tradeoffs can be identified from Figure S.2 and numerous other figures in the report.

An Example Application of Comparing Scout/Recon Systems

To exemplify using the scout/recon analysis method, we demonstrate how to compare two notional types of scout/recon systems with very different physical, operational, and technological characteristics. The systems are notional in the sense that they do not replicate existing or planned systems even though they characterize existing approaches to providing battlefield intelligence. System A features high-altitude, standoff surveillance with long-range sensors that provide an expansive, low-resolution picture of selected operations areas in the theater, including but not dedicated to the area of interest to a particular heavy division. System B represents advanced scout/recon helicopters organic to the division.

In our example, we sought to analyze how systems A and B could support a heavy division assigned to defend a designated area in terrain typical to much of the northern hemisphere, mildly rolling plains and forested low hills. Our analytical interest focused on a friendly division in a prepared defense that, because of deployment factors and prior operations, finds the division at 70% readiness; the division is under impending attack by advancing enemy tank divisions. We considered the case where the division's situation assessment cell processes information manually, and the division dedicates quick-reaction scout/recon assets that, on average, take about two hours to respond to special intelligence collection requests. We assume that the division's counterrecon capability can limit the enemy's reconnaissance units to making contact with only its forward force elements.

System A provides surveillance of the division's area of interest every three hours and reports the objects it senses to a ground facility for processing and distribution to the division through a theater intelligence network, thus the information arrives at the division situation assessment cell three hours after system A collects it. We ascribe to system A a technology that can provide detection of objects across the full range of its sensor, but cannot classify or recognize them. System A survives by operating over friendly controlled or otherwise safe territory and maintaining a standoff distance beyond the range of enemy air defense systems; hence, system A can provide NAI coverage to an average depth of 75 kilometers behind the enemy's forward trace over the course of an enemy road march.

We assumed that system B would be launched on scout/recon missions every three hours and has automatic target handoff (ATHS) capability so it can provide collected data to the situation assessment cell within five minutes of an observation. The precision of the information collected by system B results from the confluence of its sensor technology, its ability to physically position itself to bring the sensors to bear, and its survivability that results in its covering assigned NAIs 40 kilometers behind the enemy forward trace and operating in a manner that permits it to recognize enemy weapon systems.

Factor Levels for the Example

The factor levels that define the above situation for the SCRMM are shown below.

	System A	System B
Operation:		Defense
Readiness assessment:		70%
Enemy scout/recon performance:		Contact with forward force elements
Processing:		Manual
Responsiveness:		2 hours

	System A	System B
Persistence:	3 hours	3 hours
Timeliness:	2 hours	5 minutes
Precision:	Detection	Recognition
Depth:	75 kilometers	40 kilometers

Calculating and Comparing the Value of Systems A and B

The graphs in the right panel of Figure S.3 show the percent of NAIs that could be timely covered if the quick-reaction force could respond to special requests in two hours. System A's 75-kilometer depth of coverage and 3-hour persistence results in timely coverage of 40% of the essential NAIs. System B's 40-kilometer depth of coverage and 3-hour persistence results in timely coverage of 30% of the essential NAIs. Hence, system A covers a third more NAIs than does system B.

In the left panel, the graphs show the percent of key force elements that could be identified using manual situation assessment processing. The lower line reflects

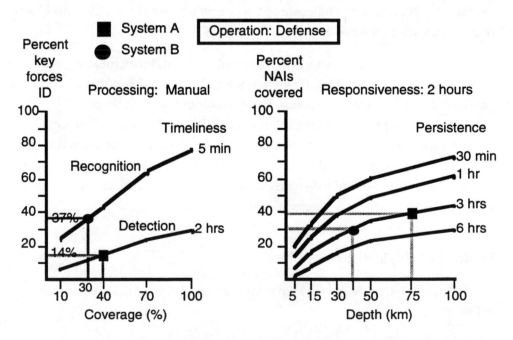

**Figure S.3—Graphical Assessment of Dissimilar Scout/Recon Assets:
Coverage and Key Elements Identified**

a *detection* precision level coupled with a 2-hour timeliness level; the upper line reflects a *recognition* precision level coupled with a 5-minute timeliness level. For system A we enter the chart at the 40% coverage determined on the right panel and, using the lower line graph, determine that with system A providing the scout/recon inputs, 14% of the key enemy force elements could be identified and tracked. Entering the chart at the 30% coverage point that system B could achieve, we see that because of system B's higher precision and near-real-time data input, 37% of the key enemy force elements could be identified and tracked.

Figure S.4 shows the percent of key enemy force elements that the division could defeat when the enemy's scout/recon forces could observe only the forwardmost friendly forces (the covering force). Each line graph represents outcomes for a different division operational readiness level. For the selected readiness of 70%, first observe that if the situation assessment capability is unable to identify any of the enemy's forces, the division could defeat slightly more than 30% of the key enemy force elements. Given the 14% identification level resulting from system A's inputs, the division could defeat 35% of the enemy key force elements; with system B, 46% could be defeated.

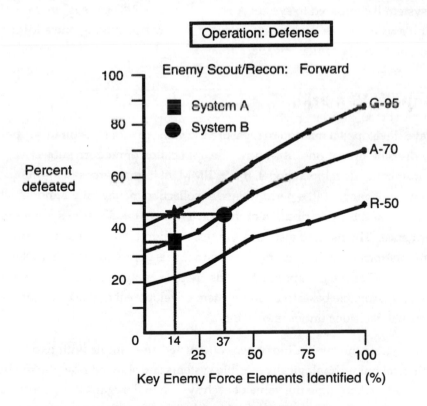

Figure S.4—Graphical Assessment of Dissimilar Scout/Recon Assets: Enemy Force Elements Defeated

Hence, the SCRMM results indicate that (1) system A's inputs result in division operational effectiveness (measured by key force elements defeated) slightly better (by one-sixth) than having no scout/recon inputs and (2) system B's inputs result in division operational effectiveness approximately one-third greater than if system A provided the scout/recon support and over one-half greater than having no scout/recon inputs.

Another perspective on these results comes from the readiness substitution concept, which interprets the difference in operations performance in terms of the difference in the division's readiness needed to achieve the same performance level. In our example, we can determine from Figure S.4 the increase from 70% readiness that would produce the same percent defeated with system A that was produced with system B (46%). Regardless of readiness level, with system A only 14% of the key enemy force elements are identified. From Figure S.4 we see that in order to defeat 46% of the enemy force elements when only 14% of them are identified, operational readiness would need to be increased from 70% to 94%. Hence, under the conditions of the example, we would conclude that the difference in a heavy division's operational effectiveness with system B compared to system A is the same as a 24% increase in the division's readiness—roughly equivalent to the division having one additional operationally ready armor brigade.

Summary Remarks

We have developed a method to measure the value of scout/recon in support of heavy division operations. It features the application of modern subjective measurement to develop a model, the SCRMM, of human processes—the division intelligence staff's performance of collection management and situation assessment, and the contribution of these activities to the division's operational performance. The method also incorporates the simulation of scout/recon system missions in high-resolution combat models to provide inputs to the SCRMM. We believe the approach yields credible analytic results and can provide a reasonable basis to inform system development and acquisition as well as doctrinal decisions under uncertainty.

To demonstrate the methodology, we constructed an example with two hypothetical but technologically feasible systems and showed how the method can be used to determine the value of each system with regard to its contribution to division operational effectiveness. In addition to directly comparing their values, we also compared them by equating their difference in value to differences in division readiness, which equates roughly to additional forces that would be required to achieve the better result—a direct connection to the force multiplier concept.

To measure the value of scout/recon in support of light force operations, the same general approach would pertain. For light forces, however, the analysis would address different combat situations that most likely would require different MOPs that depend on somewhat different processes. This would require developing appropriate operating concepts and the situation assessment and operations models that reflect those concepts in terms of both processes and MOPs. One would also need to develop and operationalize combat scenarios relevant to future worldwide light force projections and expand the military context for scout/recon to include low-intensity conflicts featuring prolonged maneuvering preceding selected combat that could include highly mobile small-unit strikes, indirect fire, and combat with less-than-leading-edge enemy forces in moderate-size battles.

1. Introduction

This report describes the development and use of a method for conducting quantitative analysis of scout-reconnaissance (scout/recon) systems that accounts for their effects on human processes in military intelligence and operations as well as the operational and technological aspects of the scout/recon mission. The method is system independent; it can be used to measure the value of any type of system conducting scout/recon. It can provide an analytically derived operational performance input to use in making decisions about developing and acquiring scout/recon systems. The method exploits expert judgment and high-resolution interactive simulation.

Background

In today's fiscally constrained budget environment, difficult decisions must be made about the development and acquisition of reconnaissance, surveillance, and target acquisition (RSTA) systems that can support ground combat operations. Competing systems having different characteristics include the joint surveillance and target acquisition radar system (JSTARS), short- and close-range unmanned aerial vehicles (UAVs), and fixed- and rotary-wing aircraft. The Army has a particular need to replace its aging fleet of low-technology, limited-capability scout helicopters.

Ground commanders include scout/recon operations as an essential element of their preparation for combat operations. They and their soldiers realize that what they know or do not know about the enemy could determine their chance of success in combat as much as how well-armed, well-trained, and ready they are to fight. Throughout military history, the collection and processing of enemy information has taken on many different forms. Scout and reconnaissance operations charged with collecting information have evolved with tactical requirements and technology to encompass ground-, air-, and space-based systems and state-of-the-art sensors. Processing also has evolved, with the aid of real-time communications, data digitization, and electronic computation. Today the evolution continues as the military seeks to gain a fighting edge on the information-age battlefield by developing increasingly effective intelligence systems, techniques, and procedures.

A longstanding problem for modern scout/recon systems development and acquisition decisionmaking has been the lack of analytical tools for measuring the operational value of scout/recon systems, concepts, and technologies. The analytical community has lagged in developing methods to quantify this contribution; hence, it has not been possible to quantitatively compare alternative systems or establish relationships between scout/recon performance and operational outcomes. Without such methodology, the assessment of these systems' contribution to combat performance has relied largely on military judgment and commanders' testimonials to the importance of scout/recon to their ability to position, maneuver, and apply their forces for successful battle outcomes. Because of the current sophistication of analytic methods for addressing military questions, this unstructured judgment has not been especially useful in debates about program alternatives.

The difficulty in conducting quantitative scout/recon analysis centers on its human process connection to operational results. Scout/recon activities generate information that a human situation assessment process uses to develop a dynamic "picture" of the enemy forces in order to support operational decisionmaking about how to fight the force; these decisions, in turn, affect battle outcomes.

Scout/Reconnaissance

When addressing scout/recon, it is necessary to consider three aspects of the overall operation that, together, provide the basis for its evaluation. First, there are the *attributes* of the scout/recon system itself.[1] These include the sensors through which the enemy's environment is observed, communications to transmit observations and to command and control the scout/recon assets, and navigation and positioning to determine the location of own and observed enemy systems. Second, for airborne systems, *flight dynamics* are critical to their ability to operate within the enemy's environment from the standpoint of endurance, range, and survivability. Third, the *signatures* of a scout/recon system (radio, radar, infrared, optical, audio) and a system's ability to counteract enemy defensive efforts importantly affect its survivability and, hence, effectiveness. These aspects of a scout/recon system determine its ability to provide intelligence inputs with some level of completeness, detail, accuracy, and timeliness.

---

[1]In this research we consider "scout/recon system" in its broadest sense to include any manned or unmanned collection system(s) operating above or on the ground supported by command, control, and communications systems and procedures.

The essence of a scout/recon system's value is not the intelligence it produces per se, but how that intelligence contributes to the intelligence staff's ability to assess the enemy's situation and, in turn, to the commander's ability to most effectively maneuver and position his forces and target the enemy's force elements. Hence, the value of scout/recon lies solely in how well it supports the human processes of situation assessment and operations decisionmaking that result in battle outcomes. An analytic method that measures this value must measure these processes in terms of their outcomes or products.

Direct recipients of scout/recon intelligence are the officers involved in assessing the enemy's situation, and those involved in targeting direct and indirect fire systems. This research focuses on situation assessment and force maneuver and positioning rather than targeting. The targeting missions performed by, for example, artillery forward observers or scout helicopters on an attack helicopter team are distinctly different from missions aimed to maintain surveillance of enemy forces. The effectiveness of the former can be assessed in the framework of existing combat models that simulate engagements and tally kills and losses (e.g., JANUS). The latter support the commander's intelligence preparation of the battlefield, his determination of the enemy's tactics and strategy, and his decisions on actions to maximize success; until now surveillance missions have lacked analytical methods for determining their value.

The Operational Backdrop

We set our research against a backdrop of heavy (armored and mechanized infantry) division operations. This choice was based on the division's central role in the conduct of battle and its role as a primary developer and user of intelligence. The division has the full range of organic combat and combat support elements, including scout/recon assets. The division staff includes a Directorate of Intelligence (G-2) and a Directorate of Operations (G-3) with full capability to employ the division's scout/recon assets, integrate their own intelligence with intelligence provided by higher echelons, perform independent assessment of the enemy activity within their area of operations, and develop and implement operational plans to achieve the division's combat objectives.

The most demanding combat situations pit modern armored units in high-intensity battle; hence we elected to consider combat operations wherein friendly armored or mechanized infantry forces either are in a prepared defense against a concerted enemy attack or are attacking a prepared enemy defense. Both operations feature approximately a three-to-one attacker to defender advantage and assume that both sides are equipped with modern combat systems and well-trained and motivated personnel.

We emphasized the battle phase in the critical final 36 hours before initial contact between the lead combat elements in the security zone. In this period, the commander and his staff seek to clarify the enemy's operational plan and intention, locate his primary fighting units and avenues of approach, and make final adjustments to the division's forces to provide the best opportunity to defeat the enemy.

The Scout/Recon Analysis Method

We used different research approaches to address the different elements of technology, military doctrine and concepts, and human information processing that all play a role in how scout/recon capabilities affect battle outcomes. We modeled the human processes using psychological measurement techniques, naming the model the Scout/Reconnaissance Measurement Model (SCRMM). We applied high-resolution, operator-interactive computer models to simulate scout/recon missions in combat scenarios to determine a scout/recon system's performance. The simulation results and other information describing a particular scout/recon system and operating environment are input to the SCRMM, which computes their effects on operational performance.

Figure 1.1 is a schematic of the scout/recon analysis method. The two primary analysis elements, the scout/recon mission simulation and the SCRMM, depend on selected information drawn from the combat scenarios that define the specific operational environments of interest to a particular scout/recon system analysis. Detailed scout/recon system characteristics, essential for accurately representing a particular system in the mission simulations, are needed to achieve credible mission results; these, as shown, are input to the SCRMM. The scout/recon system's force structure establishes the level of scout/recon activities that can be sustained, an input to the SCRMM that affects the amount of information available to the situation assessment process. The SCRMM integrates the inputs from these multiple sources and computes a measure of the scout/recon system's value in terms of operational performance.

The analysis method can account for the full range of elements that importantly affect the performance of a scout/recon system. It provides the capability to compare different scout/recon systems, extant or proposed, and to highlight scout/recon characteristics with high payoff potential.

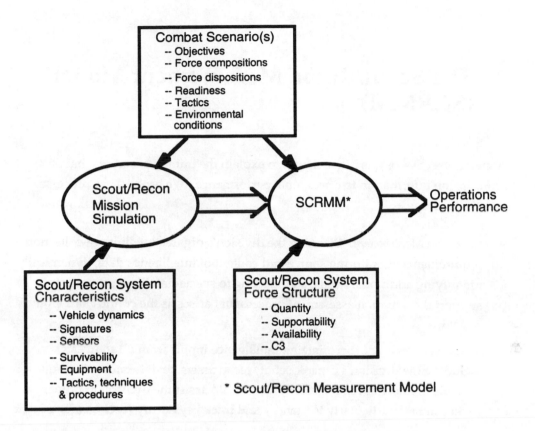

Figure 1.1—Schematic of Scout/Recon Analysis Method

Report Organization

In Section 2 we first describe our scout/recon measurement model (SCRMM) of the human processes that link scout/recon intelligence information to operational performance. We then describe how we developed this model using the STF approach, which incorporates modern psychological measurement techniques. In Section 3 we describe how scout/recon system missions would be simulated using the suite of interactive high-resolution models in RAND's Combat Analysis Environment. In Section 4 we describe how to use the SCRMM for analysis either within the framework of the overall method to measure the value of a specified scout/recon system(s) or as a stand-alone analysis tool to explore and assess notional systems or concepts and seek to identify system enhancements or tradeoffs with high marginal payoffs. In Section 5 we demonstrate by example how to use the scout/recon analysis method to compare the capabilities of different (notional) scout/recon systems in terms of operational performance.

2. The Scout/Recon Measurement Model (SCRMM)

A major objective of this research was to explain the human processes that link scout/recon information to operational performance. We broke these processes into three areas:

- *Collection Management.* Planning the division's organic intelligence-collection requirements, monitoring source and content of intelligence data, dynamically identifying additional needs, and reacting to special intelligence requests to support the situation assessment process that arises as the conflict situation develops.

- *Situation Assessment.* Scrutinizing intelligence inputs from all sources, including the division's organic scout/recon assets, to determine all things possible to know about the enemy that would assist the division in preparing to do combat, particularly to identify and track key enemy force elements.

- *Operational Performance.* The combat performance of the forces as a result of the decisionmaking processes that follow from the situation assessment input and other factors pertaining to the operational situation.

We applied the Subjective Transfer Function (STF) method (Veit and Callero, 1981; Veit, Callero, and Rose, 1984) to develop a scout/recon measurement model (SCRMM) of these three processes. The STF method was developed to analyze human-dominated systems that comprise multiple processes occurring simultaneously or sequentially. In this approach, sets of factors that define sequentially occurring processes are linked hierarchically via factors that play a dual role: they are an outcome factor (e.g., a measure of performance (MOP) factor) at one hierarchical tier and an input factor at the next-higher tier in the hierarchy. This feature can be seen in the SCRMM in Figure 2.1.

Each hierarchical tier in Figure 2.1 contains the factors associated with the human processes outlined above: collection management (lowest tier), situation assessment (middle tier), and operational performance (top tier). The hierarchies link through the measure of performance (MOP) associated with each process. Each shaded square represents the MOP for the set of factors shown below it and belongs to the set of factors that affect the MOP at the next hierarchical level. The factors shown at each tier were used to construct experimental situations for

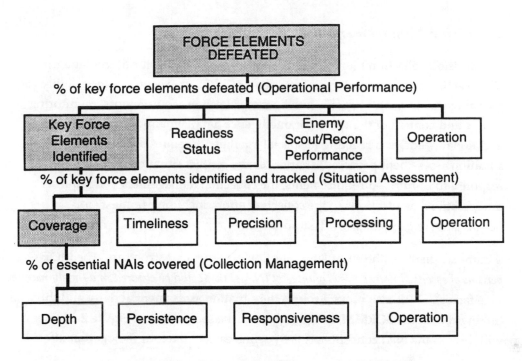

Figure 2.1—Scout/Recon Measurement Model (SCRMM)

subject matter experts (SMEs) to judge in terms of the associated MOP. SMEs' judgments were then used as the database to test among potential measurement theories of the process.

In this section we describe (a) the factors and MOPs comprising the SCRMM; (b) how the SCRMM's hierarchical structure was constructed; (c) the modern measurement framework and the determination of the subjective measurement functions (referred to as STFs once determined for each tier and functionally interlinked) that explain SME judgments and link hierarchical tiers; and (d) how to assess the value of scout/recon using the SCRMM.

The SCRMM

The overall MOP shown at the top of the SCRMM is the *percent of key enemy force elements that could be defeated* under various conditions described by the factors shown below it. The notion of "defeated" is that the unit ceases to be an effective fighting force and/or can no longer influence battle outcomes either because of friendly fire or maneuver; "key" force elements are those that importantly influence battle outcomes, such as ground maneuver units, artillery, aviation, air defenses, and reconnaissance elements. We begin our description of the factors and MOPs shown in Figure 2.1 at the lowest tier, with Collection Management, and work up to the top tier, Operational Performance.

Collection Management

The division collection management cell resides in the director of intelligence (G-2) section of the tactical operations center (TOC). It executes responsibility for planning the division's organic intelligence collection requirements, monitoring source and content of the inflow of intelligence data, dynamically identifying additional needs, and reacting to special intelligence requests to support the situation assessment process that arises as the conflict situation develops. In response to unfulfilled requirements, the collection management cell requests modifications or additions to the collection effort, including requests for nondivision (e.g., theater-level) support.

Figure 2.2 displays the complete collection management structure. The MOP was *the percent of essential named areas of interest (NAIs) that could be covered in a timely manner.* This factor, which also plays a role in the situation assessment activity and thus has a linking role in the SCRMM, is highlighted in the second tier of Figure 2.1. First we will discuss the NAI concept and then define each of the four factors that affect it.

During the intelligence preparation of the battlefield (IPB), the director of intelligence designates NAIs in locations on the battlefield thought to be important places to monitor enemy activity. The example shown in Figure 2.3 depicts the situation where friendly forces are in a prepared defense on the left and the enemy is advancing from the right to the left. The shaded areas are notional NAIs—potential river crossings (A, B, C, D), potential artillery and command post locations (E, F, G), and areas from which an attack might be launched (AA, BB)—placed along the enemy's likely avenues of advance.

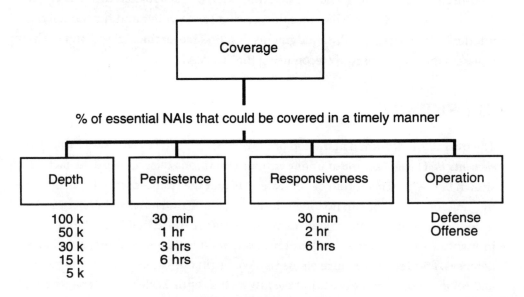

Figure 2.2—Collection Management Structure

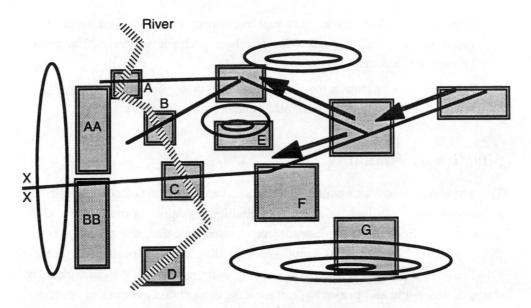

Figure 2.3—Named Areas of Interest (NAI)

Ideally, NAIs would be monitored at *all* times and enemy activity within them reported as it happens. In practice, NAIs form the mission goals of scout/recon systems and are monitored only when the scout/recon system has them under surveillance. As an enemy moves through the NAI environment, certain NAIs become "essential" for a period of time in the sense that observing and reporting the enemy activity would provide essential information to the situation assessment process, enabling it to maintain a complete picture of the enemy's movements and apparent intentions during their advance. At other times, NAIs have no important enemy activity taking place within them and, hence, are not essential.

The ability of the G-2 staff to provide the director of operations (G-3) and commander a complete picture of the enemy's positions and movement depends in large part on how well the NAIs are covered by the scout/recon system when they are essential.

Factors that affected SMEs' judged ability to timely cover NAIs are defined below. The factor levels used to construct situations used in the judgment experiments are listed after each definition.

- *Depth.* The distance behind the forward trace of the enemy's main body that information can be collected. Factor levels were 100k, 50k, 30k, 15k, and 5k.
- *Persistence.* The frequency with which information is collected at each NAI (revisit frequency). Factor levels were 30 minutes, 1 hour, 3 hours, and 6 hours.

- *Responsiveness.* The time from requesting nonscheduled reconnaissance until a collection system begins to collect the data. Factor levels were 30 minutes, 2 hours, and 6 hours.

- *Operation.* The operation the division is conducting. Factor levels were defense (i.e., prepared defense) and offense (i.e., deliberate attack).

Situation Assessment

The division situation assessment activity also resides in the G-2 section of the TOC. It executes responsibility for scrutinizing intelligence inputs from all sources, including the division's organic scout/recon assets, to determine all things possible to know about the enemy that would assist the division in preparing to do combat. This includes locating and identifying enemy units, estimating the enemy's force strength, following and projecting routes of movement and avenues of approach, and trying to understand the enemy's intentions. A basic product of this activity is a picture and description of the enemy's overall force posture and the location and description of enemy key force elements. This information provides the division commander and his operations staff the intelligence input to integrate with other information in making operational decisions.

The MOP for this process was *percent of key force elements that could be identified and tracked* during the critical decisionmaking phases of the operation. This factor is highlighted at the top tier of the SCRMM shown in Figure 2.1, indicating its function in linking the middle and top tiers of the hierarchy. The complete situation assessment structure is shown in Figure 2.4. "Key force elements" was defined here as for the MOP shown at the top of the SCRMM: elements that importantly influence battle outcomes. They include ground maneuver units, artillery, aviation, air defenses, and reconnaissance elements. To identify these key force elements meant that at least type and size had to be assessed; tracking required following the unit's location and movement. The critical decisionmaking phases referred to those times when maneuver decisions could be made that could influence outcomes. The five factors affecting this MOP and their associated factor levels used to construct situations for the judgment experiments are:

- *Coverage.* The percent of named areas of interest (NAIs) that were timely covered by the collection management cell. Factor levels were 100%, 70%, 40%, 10%, and 0%.

- *Timeliness.* Time between information collection and its availability for use by the situation assessor. Factor levels were 5 minutes, 45 minutes, 2 hours, and 6 hours.

- *Precision.* The level of detail about enemy weapon systems reported by the collection system. Levels of this factors were:
  — Recognition (discriminating within tracked and wheeled vehicles).
  — Classification (discriminating between tracked or wheeled vehicles).
  — Detection (location of objects only; no discrimination).

- *Processing.* How information is interpreted and displayed. Factor levels were:
  — Fully automated: intelligence data are entered into a computer which, based on an assessment program, makes a first-order interpretation of the enemy's situation for display to the human assessor. The human assessor integrates the automated interpretation with other available information (perhaps using the computer as in the semiautomated mode below) to make a final assessment.
  — Semiautomated: intelligence data are entered into a computer containing software that allows a broad capability for the human assessor to organize, combine, selectively scan, etc. the data and display it graphically, tabularly, or textually to support a final assessment of the enemy's situation.
  — Manual: the information is presented in hardcopy for the situation assessor to interpret and display the situation on grease boards and maps.

- *Operation.* The operation the division is conducting. Factor levels were defense and offense, as described earlier.

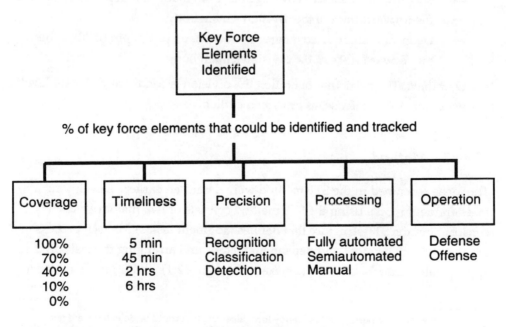

Figure 2.4—Situation Assessment Structure

Operational Performance

The MOP for the operational performance portion of the structure shown in Figure 2.1, the *percent of key force elements that could be defeated*, was defined earlier.[1] The factors and factor levels shown in Figure 2.5 used to construct the judgment experiments are defined below.

- *Percent of Key Force Elements That Were Identified and Tracked.* Factor levels were 100%, 70%, 50%, 25%, or 0%.

- *Readiness Status of Division Forces.* The division's percent readiness scale, as determined by standard Army readiness status ratings. In the context of imminent combat addressed here, readiness status is the proportion of maximum potential combat power that the division can achieve based on authorized equipment that is serviceable, personnel that are trained, and support capability required to sustain the battle; it reflects the operational readiness of each subordinate combat unit accumulated across the division. The scale goes from 0% to 100%. Factor levels were 95%, 70%, 50%, and 30%.

- *Enemy's Scout/Recon Performance.* The scout/recon operations the enemy has accomplished as a result of its capability and the division's ability to do counterreconnaissance. Factor levels were:
  — No contact has been made with division forces.
  — Contact has been made with only the forward division force elements (e.g., covering force).
  — Shallow surveillance: coverage has been made to a depth of 5k behind the forward trace of the division's main body.
  — Deep surveillance: coverage has been made to a depth of 20k behind the forward trace of the division's main body.

- *Operation.* The particular operation the division is conducting. Factor levels were defense or offense, as described earlier.

The STF Method

The ideas contained in the STF method were described earlier. Developing a measurement model using the STF method consists of two major phases: (1) constructing the STF structure that defines judgment task(s) for each process in terms of its independent and dependent factors, and arranging the tasks in their appropriate hierarchical order (for example, Figure 2.1); and (2) using modern

---

[1]Judgments of the percent of key enemy force elements that could be defeated were not restricted to a subset of the key force elements that would have been identified and tracked by the situation assessment cell but considered all key force elements in the enemy force.

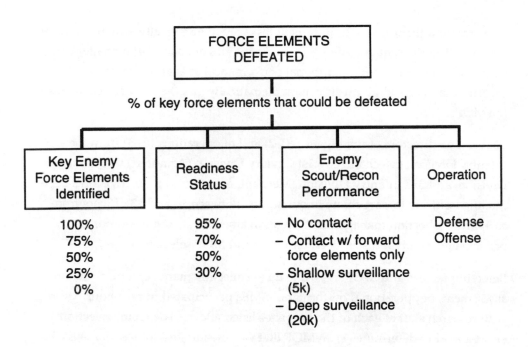

Figure 2.5—Operational Performance Structure

psychological measurement techniques to (a) design the judgment experiment(s) for each judgment task represented in the STF hierarchy, and (b) analyze judgment data after they have been collected to determine the algebraic measurement theory for each process and thus link the hierarchical processes to form the STF measurement model. The measurement theories linking the hierarchical levels are referred to as STFs because, in an analysis, subjective measurement functions (STFs) lower in the hierarchy transfer their outputs for use in subjective measurement functions at the next hierarchical level. These phases are described in the next two sections.

Constructing the SCRMM'S Hierarchical Structure

Constructing an STF structure requires a thorough understanding of the processes being modeled in terms of the factors that affect those processes and the MOPs that reflect the outputs of the processes. To that end, research staff participate in in-depth discussions with SMEs and, when possible, observe them performing their activities. Interactions with SMEs help research staff to select, define, and hierarchically organize judgment factors and MOPs so that three criteria are met: (1) judgment tasks defined by the factors and MOPs are meaningful to SMEs in terms of their activities and objectives, (2) judgment experiments can be performed at each hierarchical level using modern psychological measurement techniques to determine a SME's subjective measurement theory, and (3) judgment tasks are hierarchically structured (in this case to reflect the sequentially performed activities of collection management, situation assessment, and operational performance) so that measurement theories that pass validity tests can mathematically link the hierarchical levels via the MOPs.

SMEs. The directors of intelligence (G-2) and of operations (G-3) from the 4th Infantry Division (Mechanized), 1st Cavalry Division (Armored), 1st Armor Division, and 3rd Infantry Division (Mechanized) selected their division's best-qualified officers to participate in our study. Between 10 and 13 officers from each area, collection management, situation assessment, and operations, participated in initial discussions for factor and MOP selection.

Selecting factors and MOPs. Two to three collection management, situation assessment, or operational performance SMEs participated in two-hour sessions with research staff at each of the four sites listed above. The factor selection effort aimed to determine (1) an MOP that was meaningful in describing SMEs' job performance and an important factor to SMEs performing the activity that used their product (except for the highest performance measure in the STF model), that is, a factor that could play the dual role as independent and dependent factor in the structure, and (2) the key factors that affect SMEs' judgments of how well they could perform their activity in terms of their MOP.

Discussions between research staff and Army officers focused the officers' scrutiny on how they performed their tasks and interacted with their environment in a variety of combat situations. The combat backdrop was as described at the beginning of this section. Officers drew on their training experience and professional intellect; some had served in Operation Desert Storm and could also draw on that experience.

The lead-in statement in a session was to ask SMEs to describe in detail the activities they engaged in while performing their job. They proceeded to describe and discuss with the research staff details of their jobs as they understood them based on their training or actual combat experience. Descriptions focused on elements—situational, doctrinal, technological—they believed affected their performance, and included how changes in these elements, for example through technological advancements or changes in doctrine, might affect their job performance. As discussions proceeded, sets of seemingly salient factors emerged that research staff explored with respect to the necessity of including factors in the set and a set's completeness. This exploration included constructing questions that pitted factors against each other, for example, "If you were in a situation where you had A and B to work with, how much better (or worse) would you estimate your performance to be than if you had A and C?" These discussions aided the research staff in selecting factors and MOPs that satisfied the three STF criteria stated above, and combined with observations of SMEs performing their tasks in command-post exercises, resulted in the factors and MOPs depicted in the SCRMM model shown in Figure 2.1.[2]

Determining the STFs: Modern Subjective Measurement

Technical Discussion

The STF method employs modern subjective measurement methods to test among potential judgment theories for each process represented in an STF structure. We begin this section with an abbreviated technical discussion of modern subjective measurement to introduce the reader to the basic concepts.

Modern subjective measurement methods include Functional Measurement (Anderson, 1970, 1981), Conjoint Measurement (Krantz and Tversky, 1971; Krantz et al., 1971), and experimental designs and constraints that allow additional assumptions found with early formulations of these two approaches to be tested (Birnbaum, 1974, 1980; Birnbaum and Veit, 1974a, 1974b; Mellers, 1982; Mellers, Davis, and Birnbaum, 1984; Veit, 1978). The basic concept of modern subjective measurement is to construct experimental designs to *test* hypotheses about how people value and process information contained in situations to which they respond. Hypotheses are theories of the judgment data expressed in the form of algebraic functions. Experimental designs must allow distinction among the predictions of different theories; they must contain enough data constraints (many chances for a theory's predictions to be *wrong*) so as to allow *rejection* of incorrect theories. Thus, when a theory passes its tests, it has received empirical support for its validity as a representation of how people value and process information.

In modern subjective measurement, three transformations are postulated to occur between the time information is presented to people for judgment and a response is made: First, there is the *value function*, V (alternatively referred to as the psychophysical, psychological, or utility function) that transforms information presented for judgment into subjective values. For two pieces of information, A_i

---

[2]It is possible for factors originally hypothesized to affect SMEs' judgments to emerge as having no effect after hypotheses have been tested. Such factors would be rejected as playing a role in the STF measurement model.

16

and B_j, and their associated subjective values, s_{Ai} and s_{Bj}, his value transformation can be written

$$s_{Ai} = v_A(A_i) \tag{1}$$

$$s_{Bj} = v_B(B_j),$$

where functions V_A and V_B transform the ith level of factor A and the jth level of factor B, respectively, into their associated subjective values. Second, there is the *process function*, P, which specifies how people process their subjective values to form a subjective response, r_{ij}:

$$r_{ij} = P(s_{Ai}, s_{Bj}). \tag{2}$$

Third, there is a *judgment function*, J, that specifies how people convert their subjective responses (e.g., MOPs) into observed responses, R_{ij}:

$$R_{ij} = J(r_{ij}). \tag{3}$$

The measurement goal is to determine the algebraic form of the process function P in equation 2 (also referred to as the judgment theory or measurement theory). Once this is accomplished, the theory yields the subjective values; they are the best-fit parameter estimates given the judgment data and the theory's algebraic form.

When judgment data are obtained using experimental designs that allow tests among potential theories and J in equation 3 is linear, tests among theories can be performed directly on the data (illustrated in the data analysis section below).[3] Based on earlier support for the linearity of response dimensions (MOPs) similar to those used in the present study, we tested our theories under the assumption that the judgment transformation in equation 3 is linear.

Experimental Designs

The key to testing among potential measurement theories to explain judgments lies in the experimental design. The experimental design must contain the elements necessary to test the unique predictions of theories under contention

---

[3]If there is reason to believe the judgment function J is not linear (for example, there is evidence that the particular response scale (e.g., MOP) produces a bias—see Veit (1978), Birnbaum (1978, 1980), and Mellers, Davis, and Birnbaum (1984)), then data must be transformed according to the theorized form of J before judgment theories can be tested. Birnbaum (1982) discusses issues in testing theories on transformed data. Experimental designs that allow tests of the linearity of J are described in a number of articles. Among the earliest are those of Birnbaum (1974), Birnbaum and Veit (1974a), Birnbaum (1978, 1980), Veit (1978), and Veit, Rose, and Ware (1982).

and provide ample opportunity for the theories to be wrong. The factorial combination of factors (the procedure of crossing each level of each factor with each level of every other factor) is a prominent experimental design feature for testing among competing algebraic theories. However, this design feature alone is not sufficient for testing among some theories (e.g., adding versus averaging) that might be reasonable competitors (see Veit, Callero, and Rose, 1984). For our judgment experiments we used full factorial designs that included all factor combinations as well as smaller factorial design subsets, thus making it possible to distinguish among a number of different theories. Our experimental designs are detailed for each judgment task in Appendix A.

Data Collection Procedures

For our three experiments, respondents met in groups of three to six. A total of 23 respondents participated in the collection management judgment experiment, 27 in the situation assessment experiment, and 25 in the operational performance judgment experiment. Sessions began with a briefing. Topics covered the battle backdrop (described at the beginning of this section), including enemy and friendly force size, the MOP, and the factors hypothesized to affect it. Discussions occurred both during and following the briefing presentation on these topics and were followed by discussions of representative subsets of questionnaire situations. The purpose of the comprehensive discussions was to set the backdrop against which SMEs were to make their judgments, and to establish familiarity with the task and questionnaire format. After discussing the combat backdrop, the factors and factor levels, and the situations described in the questionnaire for about an hour, participants filled out their individual questionnaires.

Situations presented for judgment. Below we present examples of the information comprising a situation presented for judgment developed from the full factorial design.

- *Collection Management* (Figure 2.2). In the 36-hour period prior to contact, judge how many NAIs you could timely cover if you could collect information 50 kilometers behind the enemy's first trace (depth capability), you could revisit the NAIs laid out in the plan every 30 minutes (persistence capability), you could get a quick reaction force out to cover an NAI not included in the plan within 60 minutes (responsiveness capability), and your division was in a prepared defense.

- *Situation Assessment* (Figure 2.4). Judge the percentage of the key force elements you could identify and track if the collection management cell covered 40% of the NAIs in a timely manner, the information you were working with was 45 minutes old (timeliness capability) and was at the classification level (precision capability), you processed the information manually, and the division was on the offense.

- *Operational Performance* (Figure 2.5). Judge the percentage of enemy key force elements that the division could defeat if the situation assessment cell identified and tracked 75% of the key force elements, the division was at a 95% readiness status, the enemy scout/recon elements have contact only with the division's forwardmost forces, and the division was on the offense.

For all three experiments, SMEs were instructed to draw on their professional training and experience to provide their best judgment of what the MOP would be in each situation. They were further instructed to compare each situation with every other situation; that is, their responses were to reflect the *difference* one situation might make over others in the MOP outcome. The experimental situations were presented in matrix format to facilitate comparisons. The situation awareness questionnaire is presented in Appendix B for illustration purposes.

SMEs could respond to questions in any order they liked. Some respondents preferred beginning with extreme situations (best and worst) and working unsystematically towards more moderate situations; others preferred the reverse, and still others skipped around more.[4] Participants worked at their own pace, taking from one to two hours to complete their questionnaire, depending on its length and individual differences in rate of responding.

Data Analyses

The goal of our data analyses for each of the three experiments was to determine the algebraic measurement theory (the STF in the SCRMM) that explained SMEs' judgments. Our analyses for each experiment began by examining main and interaction effects of factors on judgments for each individual SME. Since SMEs within each group exhibited very similar effects (described in the next section), we averaged their data for theory testing.

First we describe our data analyses for each judgment experiment. The analysis graphs for the three judgment experiments shown in Figures 2.6 to 2.9 depict

---

[4]We have previously tested for order effects of the matrix format by comparing this format with a random ordering of questions. Since we found no effect of order in questionnaire format, we use a matrix form, since it facilitates respondents' comparisons of each situation with every other situation, and respondents fill out questionnaires more rapidly.

19

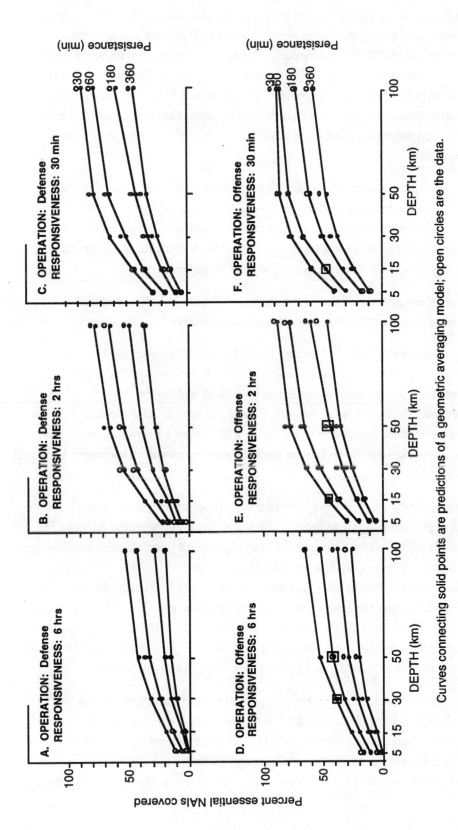

Curves connecting solid points are predictions of a geometric averaging model; open circles are the data.

Figure 2.6—Collection Management Results

both the data and the predictions of the theories selected as STFs: open circles are the data; lines connecting solid circles are the STF predictions and, thus, can be interpreted as the SMEs' perceptions. Comparison of open with solid circles provides an evaluation of how well the theories selected as STFs accounted for the effects seen in the data. The descriptions presented below on main and interaction effects in the data can be followed by attending to the curves, since the observed data points exhibit the same structure as that predicted by the STFs (described later).

After our discussions of the judgment data for each experiment, we discuss judgment theories to measure the effects seen in the data. We briefly describe theories that were rejected and then describe the theories selected as the STFs. Lastly, we present some examples of perceptual tradeoffs among factors that produce different MOP levels predicted by the SCRMM.

Collection Management. The graphs shown in the six panels of Figure 2.6 display results of the collection management data analysis.

In each panel, the percent of NAIs that could be timely covered is plotted on the y-axis as a function of Depth on the x-axis, with a separate curve for each Persistence factor level; the two left-hand panels (A and D) are for a Responsiveness level of 6 hours, middle panels are for a Responsiveness level of 3 hours, and the two right-hand panels (C and F) are for a Responsiveness level of 30 minutes. Panels A–C on top are for a defensive operation; the lower D–F panels are for an offensive operation.

The effect of Depth can be seen by the positive slopes of the curves in each panel; the effect of Persistence can be seen by the separations between the curves. The upward shift of the curves from left-hand to right-hand panels illustrates the effect of Responsiveness. A divergent interaction can be viewed in all six panels, that is, the Persistence capability (the ability to revisit NAIs) made *less* of a difference with respect to the percent of NAIs that could be timely covered when it was possible to collect information only 5k beyond the enemy's first trace than when that capability was increased to 50k or 100k (compare the vertical distances among curves at depths of 5k and 50k, respectively, in all panels).

Situation Assessment. The graphic analyses of the situation assessment SME data are shown in Figures 2.7 and 2.8. In all panels of these two figures, the percent of key enemy force elements that could be identified and tracked is plotted on the y-axis as a function of Coverage on the x-axis; a separate curve is for each Timeliness factor level. From left to right at any given row of graphs,

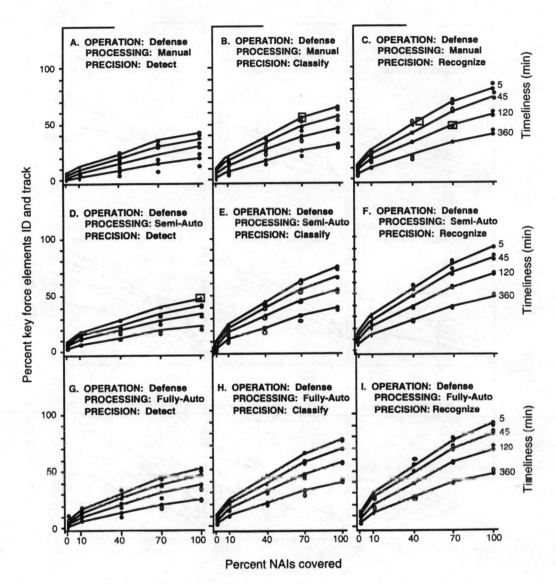

Curves connecting solid points are predictions of a geometric averaging
model; open circles are the data.

Figure 2.7—Situation Assessment Results: Friendlies Are in a Prepared Defense

changes are in level of Precision—detection, classification, and recognition. Each
row of graphs in each figure is for a different level of processing capability; from
top to bottom they are manual, semiautomated, and fully automated. All panels
in Figure 2.7 are for the case when the division is on the defense; all panels in
Figure 2.8 are for the case when the division is on the offense.

22

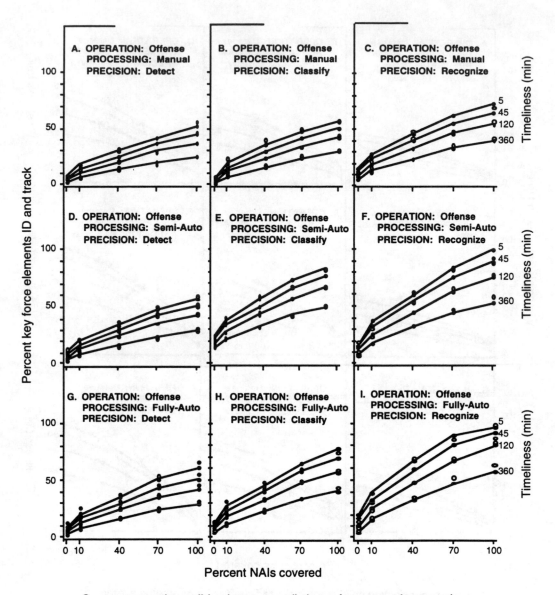

Curves connecting solid points are predictions of a geometric averaging
model; open circles are the data.

**Figure 2.8—Situation Assessment Results: Friendlies Are in an
Offensive Mode of Operation**

In each panel, the slopes of the curves illustrate the effect of Coverage; separations
between the curves the effect of Timeliness. As Precision capability increases from
Detection to Recognition (from the left-hand to the right-hand panel within any
row), the curves not only shift upward but their slopes steepen and the curves

spread apart, indicating that the effect of the Coverage/Timeliness interaction depends on the level of Precision. In all three panels within any row, having a poor or good Timeliness capability doesn't make much of a difference when only 10% of the NAIs have been covered; however, Timeliness makes more of a difference as the coverage capability increases (note that the vertical spread of the curves increases as the value on the x-axis increases). This interaction effect was seen for all factors: as the capability on one dimension improves, other dimensions are perceived to make more of a difference in SMEs' ability to identify and track key enemy force elements.

When Precision is only at the detection level, the percent of key force elements identified and tracked is low, regardless of the Timeliness or Coverage capability. The best performance is about 40% when information is close to real time (5 minutes) and NAI coverage is 100%. Big improvements are predicted when Precision is increased to Recognition.

The difference in SMEs' perceived ability to identify key force elements when on the offense versus the defense can be seen by comparing each panel in Figure 2.7 with its corresponding panel in Figure 2.8. Overall, SMEs perceived they would identify and track more targets when on the offense than when on the defense.

Operational Performance. The eight panels shown in Figure 2.9 graph the percent of key enemy force elements that could be defeated on the y-axis, as a function of the percent of enemy force elements that had been identified and tracked by the situation assessment cell on the x-axis; a separate curve is for each level of the division's readiness status, and a separate panel within each row is for a different level of enemy reconnaissance capability, from deep surveillance in the leftmost panel of each row to no surveillance in the rightmost panel. The four panels of data in the top row represent the division's situation when in a prepared defense, the four in the bottom row when the division is on the offense.

The main effects of all the factors can be viewed from the graphs. The slopes of the curves in each of the panels in Figures 2.7 and 2.8 represent the effect of the number of key enemy force elements that could be identified and tracked by the situation assessment cell; separations between the curves represent the effect of the readiness status. The upward positioning of the curves from the leftmost to rightmost panel in both rows indicates the effect of enemy reconnaissance capability. Overall, SMEs thought they could do better when on the defense than when on the offense.

As with the collection management and situation assessment judgments, divergent interactions throughout these data indicated that factors made more of

24

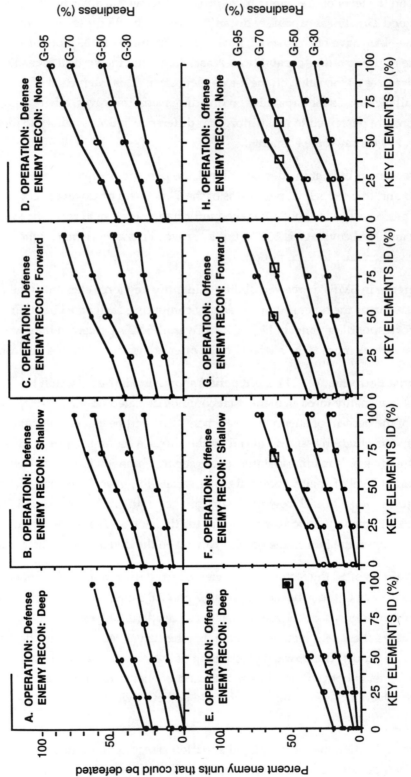

Curves connecting solid points are predictions of a geometric averaging model; open circles are the data.

Figure 2.9—Results of Operational Performance Analysis

a difference at higher levels or greater capabilities of the other factors, seen most easily in these graphs for the readiness status factor. In all of the panels, the division's readiness status doesn't make as much of a difference in defeating enemy units when the percentage of key force elements identified is 25% as when it is 100% (compare the vertical separations between the curves at 25% and 100% on the x-axis).

Perceptually, there is a greater difference between a readiness status of 70% and 50% than a readiness status of 95% and 70% or a readiness status of 50% and 30% (see the greater separation between the curves in each panel between 70% and 50% than for any other two adjacent readiness status levels). The operational performance STF predicts defeat of nearly 100% of the enemy key force elements when: the division is on the defense, 100% of the key enemy force elements have been identified and tracked, and the enemy has not had any scout/recon contact with division forces (top point in Figure 2.7D). Even if the enemy has had contact with the forward elements and only 75% of the key enemy force elements have been identified and tracked, the STF predicts defeat of about 87% of the enemy key force elements with a readiness status level of 95% (top point in Figure 2.9C).

Determining the STFs

Below we discuss the judgment theories we entertained as the STF for each human process depicted in the SCRMM shown in Figure 2.1. We discuss why we rejected the theories we rejected, and why we accepted the geometric averaging model as the measurement theory (STF) for all three processes—collection management, situation assessment, and operational performance.

Measurement theories that were rejected. The interactions shown in Figures 2.6 to 2.9 ruled out any theory that predicted independence among the factors, for example, an additive or averaging model. This class of models that predicts independence among factors predicts that the curves in Figures 2.6–2.9 should be parallel; that is, the vertical distance between any two curves should be the same, independent of the value on the x-axis.

A configural-weight or multiplicative theory can account for divergent interactions such as those seen in Figures 2.6 through 2.9. The configural-weight theory[5] has been successful in the past for accounting for SMEs' judgments in both military and social domains (for example, Veit et al., 1980; Veit, Callero, and Rose, 1982; Birnbaum, et al., 1971; Birnbaum, 1974; Birnbaum and Sotoodeh, 1991) and has recently achieved success in accounting for risky choices where other theories have failed (for example, Birnbaum et al., 1992; Weber et al., 1992). A configural-weight theory and multiplicative theory were each tested on the collection management, situation assessment, and operational performance data. These theories differ in their predictions with respect to the rank order the data points (open circles) in Figures 2.6 through 2.9 should have, and their predictions are different from the rank order seen in the data.[6] Systematic deviations from the data were found for both theories. Their average squared data/theory deviations were 21% for the configural-weight theory and 16% for the multiplicative theory across all three sets of data. Both theories and their parameter values were rejected.

The geometric averaging theory. A geometric averaging theory gave a good explanation of all three sets of data—collection management, situation assessment, and operational performance—with different sets of parameter values for each set.

The connected solid points shown in Figures 2.6–2.9 are the values predicted by the geometric averaging theory. These predictions were computed using the subjective scale values and weights derived from that theory separately for each set of judgment data.[7] As can be seen in Figures 2.6–2.9, the divergent

---

[5]A configural-weight theory can be written for three factors, A, B, and C, as follows:

$$R_{ijk} = a\left[(w_0 s_0 + w_A s_{Ai} + w_B s_{Bj} + w_C s_{Ck}) / \Sigma w + \omega(s_{MAX} - s_{MIN})\right] + b \ ,$$

where w_0 and s_0 are the weights and scale values associated with the initial impression (what the response would be in the absence of specific information); w_A, w_B, and w_C are the subjective weights associated with factors A, B, and C, respectively; Σw is the sum of these weights, and s_{Ai}, s_{Bj}, and s_{Ck} are the subjective scale values associated with the ith level of factor A, the jth level of factor B, and the kth level of factor C, respectively; s_{MAX} and s_{MIN} are the highest- and lowest-valued pieces of information, respectively, in a set, and ω is the weighting factor for this range term; and a and b are linear constants.

[6]The advantage of using factorial experimental designs is that the order of the resulting judgment data will be restricted. This constraint on the data's order can be seen in Figures 2.6–2.9. Each data point (open circle) has a rank order with respect to the other data points in the experimental set. The fact that the magnitude of the data points cannot be changed by much without altering this rank order indicates the tightness of the constraints placed on the data's order by our experimental designs. These constraints make it possible to reject theories based on a comparison of the data's order and the order predicted by the theory being tested, since different judgment theories predict different orderings.

[7]In modern measurement, theoretical parameters are derived from the data in accord with the theory rather than determined in some manner outside of the theoretical framework. We derived the best-fit parameter values for the geometric averaging model from the collection management, situation assessment, and operational performance judgment data separately, so as to minimize the sum-of-squared deviations of predicted and obtained values. This same criterion, applied to other viable judgment theories, produced predicted curves that did not follow the structure of the obtained data shown in Figures 2.6–2.9.

interactions or dependent effects of factors found throughout all three sets of data are consistent with a geometric averaging theory, as are the increasing slopes of the curves from left to right across each row of panels and from top to bottom across each column of panels. The ability of this theory to explain the data can be seen by comparing open circles (judgment data) with filled circles (theoretical predictions). This theory accounted for systematic deviations found with the configural-weight and multiplicative theories; the rank order of the data is very close to that predicted by the geometric averaging theory. The average squared data/theory discrepancy for this theory was less than 5% across all three sets of data.

The geometric averaging model states that people multiply scale values associated with judged information. But these scale values are first adjusted in their exponent by the weights people place on the factor dimensions, thus producing a nonlinear relationship between the scale value and response. The general form of this model for three variables is as follows:

$$R_{ij} = m[(s_0)^d (s_{Ai})^a (s_{Bj})^b (s_{Ck})^c] + n, \tag{4}$$

where R_{ij} is the response, s_0 is the scale value associated with the initial impression (what the response would be in the absence of specific information provided by the factor levels), and s_{Ai}, s_{Bj}, and s_{Ck} are the subjective scale values associated with the factor levels of factors A, B, and C, respectively. The exponents, a, b, c, and d are proportionate to the subjective weight placed on its factor dimension: $d = w_0 / \Sigma w$, $a = w_A / \Sigma w$, $b = w_B / \Sigma w$, and $c = w_C / \Sigma w$, where w_0 is the weight placed on the initial impression (described above), w_A, w_B, and w_C are the subjective weights associated with factors A, B, and C, respectively, Σw is the sum of these weights, and m and n are constants.

The geometric averaging theory predicts numerous tradeoffs among factors such as those described earlier in the data analyses section. These tradeoffs can be visually determined from the graphs shown in Figures 2.6 through 2.9. The theory provides subjective values along an entire physical continuum (e.g., responsiveness, timeliness, readiness status). Thus, all points along the curves for these factors can be considered in assessing tradeoffs in their effects on MOPs.

Functional Integration

The three geometric averaging theories that differed in their parameter values for each human process—collection management, situation assessment, and operational performance—were functionally integrated to form the SCRMM. The SCRMM was automated to produce an easy-to-use program for assessing the effects of different scout/recon and intelligence system capabilities on MOPs. Users can select factor levels throughout the structure to define systems and conditions of interest and evaluate resulting differences in MOPs.

3. Scout/Reconnaissance Mission Simulation

A major feature of the scout/recon analysis method is to determine scout/recon system performance by simulating scout/recon missions in high-resolution, operator-interactive combat models capable of accurately representing the important characteristics of scout/recon systems and the operational environment. These simulations directly determine two factors for input to the SCRMM: the **depth** with which the system could penetrate behind the enemy's forward trace to gather intelligence information, and the level of **precision** (detection, classification, or recognition) of that information. These two factors are seen in the SCRMM (Figure 2.1); depth is at the lowest hierarchical level and precision is at the middle level. Results of these simulated missions for different scout/recon systems provide their respective factor-level inputs to the SCRMM for analysis purposes. In addition to producing inputs to the SCRMM, scout/recon mission simulations provide for assessment of tactics, techniques, and procedures with respect to mission accomplishment and system **survivability**.

The approach does not depend on any particular mission simulator so long as the simulator can account for the important features of the scout/recon system and the interactions the system has with the combat environment. For our research, we used the suite of high-resolution, interfaced models in RAND's Combat Analysis Environment (CAE) that provide the capability for operators to interactively conduct scout/recon missions against maneuvering enemy forces. The CAE models are designed to incorporate and apply detailed representations of a scout/recon system's characteristics so that the operator conducts the missions within the capabilities and limitations afforded by the particular system being investigated. The CAE models allow representations of multiple, independently selectable and controllable sensors (e.g., FLIR, TV, radar, eyeball), dynamic operator specification of sensor fields-of-view, and manual or automatic scan capability. Other representations include aircraft survivability equipment, radar and thermal signatures, physical dimensions of the systems, and detailed flight dynamics models for each simulated aircraft. An overview of the CAE is contained in Appendix C.

In this section, as a guide to the general scout/recon mission simulation process, we briefly describe how we structured and conducted exploratory missions and represented scout/recon system characteristics in the CAE. Similar procedures would apply in principle to any simulation system. For any particular application of the approach, the procedures and representations used in the mission simulations would be tailored to the specific systems and operational environments of interest.

Research Scenarios

To assess a scout/recon system's performance, it is desirable to simulate its operations in several combat environments relevant to the intended employment of the system. In keeping with the focus of this research on combat between units equipped with modern armor, assessment of a system's performance against armored forces in rolling, hilly, and mountainous terrains is appropriate since they produce different operational opportunities and risks, and require different tactics. Rolling terrain provides long lines-of-sight (LOS) for scout/recon systems at low altitudes and for the threat defense systems. Operations in hilly terrain and mountains require different tactics than rolling terrain to overcome the difficulty of obtaining and maintaining LOS, especially at long range, and the threat systems have a similar difficulty with LOS. Also, operations at high mountainous elevations pose maneuver restrictions on flying systems which could affect their performance.

For our research, to confirm the suitability of our analytical approach, we constructed ground maneuver scenarios both in rolling and in hilly, forested terrain in the CAE. For each of these terrains, we developed three "snapshots" of a road march by an enemy moving to perform a deliberate attack against a division-sized friendly armored force. The snapshots were spaced over the 36-hour period; two represented the force distributed on three parallel avenues of approach extended approximately 75 kilometers in depth and one represented their movement into battle formation just prior to initial contact. In each representation, enemy air defense units were assumed to be using leapfrog tactics to provide coverage over the entire main body of the march. For the friendly force offensive operation, we developed a representative enemy-prepared defense laydown that featured concentrated forces with dense air defense units protecting the defenders' front and flanks.

In preparation for investigating scout/recon systems operating against the force laydowns in the scenarios, Army intelligence specialists identified NAIs that they considered appropriate to the battle condition and terrain.

Representing Scout/Recon System Characteristics

With regard to mission performance, the primary scout/recon system characteristics are its sensor suite, survival technology, signatures, and, if the system is an aircraft, flight dynamics. Here we discuss characteristics that must be specified for aircraft systems and briefly summarize how they would be considered for other types of systems.

Sensor Suites

The sensors that contribute to finding and processing enemy weapon systems are the pilot's eyesight, a FLIR, an electro-optical enhanced television system, and, for certain advanced-technology systems, a millimeter-wave fire-control radar. In the CAE, each of these sensors has operator-selectable parameters that, together, determine its contribution to finding and understanding the characteristics of objects on the battlefield. *Field-of-view*, the angular width from the centerline of where it is aimed, circumscribes a sensor's instantaneous sensing area. Field-of-view affects both the sensor's coverage at any instant and how well the scenes it observes can be resolved. The wider the field-of-view, the less the resolution of the sensor's images, hence the lower the chance that an object can be "extracted" from its surroundings. On the other hand, a narrow field-of-view complicates the overall search operation by presenting a smaller instantaneous scene. *Field-of-regard* is the total angular width of a sensor's viewing pattern taking into account the sensor's freedom of movement; an operator can point it within its movement limits.

In manual scout/recon procedures with FLIR or TV sensors, pilots typically search for indications of or actually detect objects by moving the sensor within its field-of-regard using a wide field-of-view; they then convert to a narrow field-of-view to confirm a detection and classify, recognize, or identify it, as possible. *Automated scan and target classification* refers to the capability of a sensor system to, under operator direction, automatically scan a selected area, electronically collect and process what it observes, and present to the operator a preliminary determination of the objects within its scan pattern.[1] The capability to detect, classify, recognize, or identify militarily significant objects depends largely on sensor technology and varies with distance to the object, clutter surrounding the object, and atmospheric and light conditions.

---

[1]Both the second-generation FLIR being developed for the Comanche and the Longbow fire-control system being installed on the Apache have automated scan and target classification capability.

In the CAE, each sensor is independently selectable and controllable by the operator during the mission, including specification of fields-of-view that provide ranges for detection, classification, and recognition corresponding to simulated atmospheric and clutter conditions.[2] Automatic scan capability can also be specified and controlled by the operator. In all sensor operations, the operator is responsible for maintaining line-of-sight with the search area for a sufficient period of time to complete the (simulated) task, such as automatic scan or manual search and detection followed by classification or recognition of an object.

In addition to aircraft sensor systems, similar characteristics can be represented for ground-based or high-altitude systems and used in the same way by an operator. For example, for overhead unmanned aerial vehicles, theater, or national systems, a sensor's field-of-view can proscribe a circular or elliptical pattern on the terrain that the operator can control with regard to where it is pointing and which field-of-view applies.

Survival Equipment

Two types of aircraft survival equipment can be represented and used in the CAE, radar warning and air defense system jamming. Radar warning information is presented visually to the pilot in an increasing amount of detail including (1) the fact that a radar is within line-of-sight and range, (2) the bearing to the radar, (3) the distance to the radar, and (4) the type of air defense system associated with the radar. The level of detail presented to the pilot can be set to include no radar warning at all, depending on the level of technology that is relevant to the scout/recon system. On receipt of a radar warning, the pilot can react by altering the flight path or implementing maneuvers in a manner deemed most appropriate to the operational situation.

Radar and infrared jamming capability data that reflect the capability assumed available to the aircraft is input to the air defense model, RJARS, along with the conditions under which a pilot would jam an air defense system and the jamming tactics used. As RJARS calculates aircraft survivability, the jamming specifications can affect air defense system detection, tracking, engagement, and

---

[2]This capability refers to the specification of deterministic (fixed) range/outcome specification, a technique that provides for efficient involvement of human operators. CAGIS (described in Appendix C) also permits using sensor models (see Figure 3.1) that provide the probability of detecting, classifying, etc. an object that falls within the sensor's field-of-view, the final result being determined by Monte Carlo methods.

probability of kill depending on the susceptibility of the air defense systems or their weapons to the jamming.

Signatures

Scout/recon systems' signatures affect their survivability. The CAE air defense model, RJARS, uses radar cross section and thermal emission patterns to calculate the effectiveness of radar- and IR-based air defense systems, respectively. It also uses the physical dimensions of the aircraft for optically based systems, including aided and unaided eyesight. Highly detailed radar cross section and thermal emission data are maintained in RJARS; a data entry is stored for each 10 degrees horizontally and vertically on the sphere around the air frame, thus enabling continuous calculations across the dynamically changing aspects presented to the air defense system as the aircraft "flies" its mission.

Flight Dynamics

Detailed flight dynamics data are incorporated in the CAE and used to accurately represent three-dimensional flight segments selected by the pilots during flight-profile generation. Aircraft-specific flight dynamics assure the feasibility of the flight segments so that simulated aerial maneuvers do not exceed the agility and maneuverability of the simulated aircraft. Currently the CAE contains the flight dynamics data for several Army scout/recon—capable aircraft, including the RAH-66, RAH-66 with Longbow fire control radar, AH-64A, AH-64D with Longbow fire control radar, OH-58D, and the Hunter and Eagle Eye unmanned aerial vehicles.

The Exploratory Scout/Recon Missions

Army scout helicopter pilots "flew" a set of scout/recon missions using the CAE Helicopter Flight Profile system with simulated scout/recon helicopters having modern technological features. They used nap-of-the-earth tactics to take advantage of terrain and foliage for masking. The pilots were given a premission briefing covering general posture, location, and movement of the enemy forces and the NAIs they were to cover. Based on this information, the pilots planned their missions with the goal of covering the NAIs as deeply as possible behind the enemy forward trace, so that observations of enemy forces were at the highest level of precision the operational situation would permit.

Night, clear-weather conditions were assumed. The pilots were responsible for flying in a manner consistent with night operations, using a pilot's night vision system (PNVS) for flight control, with respect to speed, obstacle clearance, and altitude above the surface. The primary simulated sensor was a controllable forward-looking infrared (FLIR) sensor with automatic sweep and image storage and recall capability for target processing. A pilot's responsibility also included maintaining LOS for a sufficient time for sensor operation during mission maneuvers, e.g., remaining unmasked long enough to complete FLIR detection of targets.

During the mission, the pilots reacted to what they saw visually or with sensors and to what their survival equipment (e.g., radar warning) indicated; they employed scout/recon tactics and doctrine applicable to scout/recon aircraft and their perceived threat situation. All sightings and defense encounters were recorded and reported. When multiple aircraft were scouting, all information about the enemy formations and air defenses obtained by any scout/recon aircraft was provided to all pilots.

After each mission, the mission profile was processed by the air defense model (RJARS) to determine the outcomes of interactions with air defense systems and aircraft survivability throughout the mission.

The exploratory missions confirmed the feasibility of using high-resolution, interactive models to simulate scout/recon missions. The pilots who participated in the missions adapted readily to the CAE's mission and flight procedures and to its simulation artificialities and were satisfied that the mission results were credible. Although our exploratory missions represented scout helicopter operations, ground scout/recon teams and systems, or overhead systems, could have been represented as well. It is important to keep in mind the "system-independent" concept underlying the method. Specific systems come into play only by defining and specifying their technical, tactical, and operational characteristics.

Tactics, Survival, and Mission Performance

Proper use of any simulation system demands that the scout/recon system's operation adhere to specified tactics, techniques, and procedures (doctrinal or experiential) appropriate for the real system to ensure that its performance with regard to survivability, depth, and precision in the simulated missions provides credible results and that credible comparisons can be made among different scout/recon systems. However, this does not imply that new tactics, techniques, and procedures should not be explored using the simulation to investigate ways to improve operational effectiveness. If the resulting approaches survive real-world operational tests and evaluations, then they can be appropriately employed to assess a scout/recon system's effectiveness under the new conditions. But operators should avoid biasing the results by "gaming" the vulnerabilities of the models or scenarios to deliberately achieve high simulation marks.

Clearly, a system's ability to survive is critical to mission accomplishment in the absolute sense that if the system cannot survive or sustains unacceptably high attrition in the operating environment it is not a viable scout/recon alternative. Furthermore, the tactics the system must use *in order to survive* can have a dominant effect on its depth of coverage and on the precision level of the information it can obtain. If survival requirements seriously hamper movement and maneuver of a system operating behind enemy lines, it would take that system longer to approach and observe each NAI, thereby affecting how much territory could be reconnoitered in any given amount of time, e.g., for rotary-wing systems, before the system must terminate the mission to refuel. Hence, a clear tradeoff emerges between depth and precision. Achieving greater depth often requires lesser attention to classifying or recognizing the weapon system detected. Classifying/recognizing may require cautious positioning for masking and attaining clear lines-of-sight, and extended observation to focus on each detected object. These types of maneuvers consume time and fuel, reducing the depth that mission endurance will allow.

Consider as well the potential conflict between precision and survivability that stems from the fact that, typically, classification requires closer positioning to the enemy forces than detection, and recognition even closer. Often, although not always, the closer the scout/recon system is to the enemy forces, the more likely it is to be engaged by enemy air defenses. Hence, prudent survival tactics may preclude the system from approaching defended enemy systems close enough to recognize or classify them, or even to detect them in the first place. Systems with high signatures, poor sensors, or full exposure requirements (to clear their sensor lines-of-sight) could be particularly vulnerable and forced to settle for lower precision inputs in order to achieve an acceptable survivability rate.

Finally, survival affects the broader issue of force management that would affect the **persistence** level that could be maintained if the scout/recon assets are attrited.

4. Applying the Method

There are a number of applications for the scout/recon analysis method with regard to measuring the value of scout/recon. The principal measurement instrument, the SCRMM, can be used for analysis either within the framework of the overall method to measure the value of a specified scout/recon system(s) or as a stand-alone analysis tool to explore and assess notional systems or concepts and seek to identify system enhancements or tradeoffs with high marginal payoffs.

In all applications, the user is responsible to determine the factor levels for input to the SCRMM and to comprehend and interpret the analytic measures the method produces. When evaluating a specified scout/recon system(s), the user must design the overall analytical approach and define: (1) the operational environments and combat scenarios of interest; (2) the technical and tactical characteristics of the scout/recon and other weapon systems (e.g., air defenses); (3) all relevant information about the friendly and enemy forces (structure, readiness, availability, etc.) needed to satisfy combat scenario development and scout/recon mission simulations; and (4) similar information needed to determine the levels for SCRMM factors that do not depend on the simulation results. The user must also select a combat simulation model within which the scout/recon missions can be credibly simulated with respect to the features of the scout/recon system, system interactions, and the tactics, techniques, and procedures that would be employed. Finally, users must meaningfully relate the results obtained from the method to the purpose of their analysis in the context of the design and implementation of their research approach.

Analytic Measures

The SCRMM's highest measurement factor, the one that indicates contribution to a heavy division's operational effectiveness, is **key force elements defeated** (the percent of key enemy force elements that the division could defeat). Additional measures of interest pertaining to the performance of the intelligence gathering and assessment processes are **key force elements identified** (the percent of key enemy force elements that could be identified and tracked) and **coverage** (the percent of essential NAIs that could be timely covered). The latter two measures provide a means to identify and assess preferred initiatives to improve the division's intelligence capability as an independent endeavor, to include enhancements to the scout/recon systems, communications systems and procedures, and internal information processing capability. The higher-level operational effectiveness measure then provides the means to consider improvements in relation to how they affect the division's overall fighting ability and compare intelligence enhancements with other approaches to achieving similar improvements such as greater emphasis on counterreconnaissance or maintaining higher states of division readiness.

Because of its general usage, commonality, and historical significance in assessing a division's fighting potential, operational readiness provides an important comparison alternative for analyzing relative contributions of different scout/recon or other division intelligence systems. The concept is to determine what change in readiness level would be required (in the judgments of the SMEs modeled by the SCRMM) to achieve the same difference in percent of key enemy force elements defeated that resulted from different scout/recon or intelligence system capabilities. This change in readiness provides a useful measure to compare the different systems' contributions to heavy division combat capability. We call this concept **readiness substitution**.

Determining Factor Levels

In order to compute the SCRMM, factor levels must be determined for each factor in the hierarchical structure shown in Figure 4.1. The gray-shaded boxes indicate the analytic measures (MOPs) that are generated by the STFs. The diagonally slashed boxes indicate factors whose levels are drawn from a combat scenario within which a scout/recon system would be analyzed. The operation is either offense or defense; the same operation needs to specified at each hierarchical level. The division's operational readiness status can be selected to reflect some expected readiness rate achieved by heavy divisions, the effect of enemy prebattle operations (e.g., air strikes or artillery barrages), or a readiness status that heavy divisions may typically be able to achieve given particular support levels.[1] Finally, the means by which the situation assessment cell does data processing comes directly from the assumptions of the technology and equipment available to the heavy division; this factor provides a means to assess the effect of computer system upgrades in the information age.

---

[1]The support levels result from policy decisions or options under consideration and may well be candidates for sensitivity analyses; nonetheless, the levels should be resolved within the assumptions of the scenario.

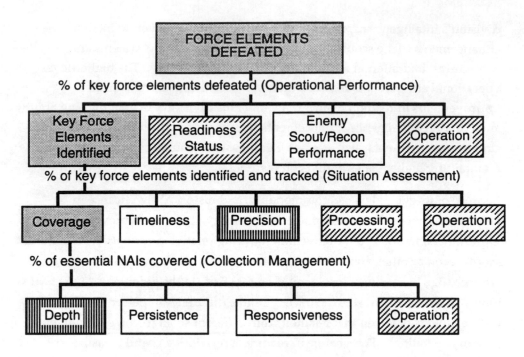

Figure 4.1—Scout/Recon Measurement Model (SCRMM)

Enemy Scout/Recon Performance

A factor level for the effectiveness of enemy scout/recon systems to find and maintain surveillance on friendly forces can reflect more than a direct assumption about enemy-system capabilities. It could result from considered judgment or combat simulations of counterreconnaissance where friendly scout/recon systems of interest may have varying capabilities to play counterreconnaissance roles that limit the enemy's ability to scout and reconnoiter friendly positions. This factor also provides a means to directly assess the effect of counterreconnaissance on battle outcomes.

Timeliness

The timeliness of the information available to assess the enemy's situation depends both on the technique used by the scout/recon system to communicate its findings back to the division and the means by which the information is processed once it arrives. For example, the time between when an observation was made and when it is available to the situation assessment cell (our definition of timeliness) is more likely to be greater if the scout/recon system must manually determine sighting locations and verbally transmit them (perhaps via communication relay nodes) than if its sighting information is electronically determined and immediately transmitted, such as could be the case with the automatic target handoff system (ATHS) now being installed on advanced helicopters. However, if the processing capability at the division does not have the capacity to process heavy volumes of real-time information, such as today's manual systems, then the overall timeliness of information from a high-technology scout/recon system certainly fails to meet its real-time potential.

Persistence

The persistence of coverage in the operating area defines how frequently the scout/recon system visits the assigned NAIs. For airborne scout/recon systems organic to the division, persistence depends on the ability of the division to generate flights. For example, in the 36-hour period relevant to this study, a persistence of 3 hours would require that the division fly 13 scout/recon missions; 4 hours would require 10 missions. The ability of the division to generate missions depends on a number of factors, including the number of scout/recon aircraft available, the programmed wartime flying hour rates, the number of aircraft required per mission, and the length of mission. The number of scout/recon aircraft available depends both on the absolute number of that type aircraft assigned to the division and the proportion of those that the division would commit to the scout/recon mission during the 36 hours of interest.[2] Hence, both unit strength and assumptions on alternate use must be considered.

Programmed wartime flying hour rates establish a bound on the number of flights the division can generate over the 36-hour period.[3] The length of the scout/recon mission and the number of aircraft on each mission play important roles. For example, a division road march on a three-road network axis of advance may cover 30 kilometers flank to flank and extend for 75 to 100 kilometers. Covering such an expansive area could consume more than the entire single mission operating endurance of the scout helicopter and may require two teams to cover the road march at each revisit time. Typically, a scout/recon team is composed of three aircraft: two to perform the scout/recon role and one to overwatch to protect them.[4]

---

[2]Competing missions for scout/recon–capable aircraft include flank security, targeting for artillery, and scouting for attack helicopter teams, all of which could be required during this period prior to contact between ground units in the security zone.

[3]While "surge" operations could increase the number of flights for a short period, the price of seriously reduced numbers of flights in the aftermath of a surge normally must be considered against the use of these same assets once the battle begins.

[4]Currently, an attack helicopter performs the overwatch mission for unarmed scout aircraft. The advent of the armed scout helicopter (Comanche, Kiowa Warrior, and even the Apache used in a scout role) may alter the three-aircraft configuration, although such a doctrinal change has not yet occurred.

Consolidating these considerations with respect to wartime flying hour rates, we see that a three-hour persistence calling for 13 missions, with each mission consisting of two teams of three aircraft, would require $6 \times 13 = 78$ flights. If a 24-aircraft air cavalry squadron was dedicated, the 78 flights would result in an average of 3.25 missions per aircraft during the 36-hour period: a rate of 2.17 missions per day. If missions lasted one hour and forty-five minutes, average flight time per aircraft would be five hours and forty-one minutes, so the cavalry squadron's daily flying hour rate would have to be at least three hours and forty-eight minutes per aircraft.

More generally, the following equation calculates persistence based on operations and support factors.

$$\text{Persistence} = \frac{T}{\dfrac{(T/24) \times N \times R}{S \times D} - 1},$$

where

T = the time span between the first and last scout/recon mission launch
(in our example T = 36, i.e., first launch at time 0, last launch at time 36);

N = the number of scout/recon aircraft dedicated to the mission
(in our example N = 24);

R = the wartime (or surge) daily flying hour rate per aircraft
(in our example R = 3.8 hours);

S = the mission size, i.e., the number of aircraft on each mission
(in our example S = 6);

D = the duration (length) of a scout/recon mission
(in our example D = 1.75 hours).

This discussion indicates how to determine persistence for scout/recon helicopters. To determine persistence for a ground-based scout/recon system, such as a long-range patrol team, assumptions about tactics and procedures would need to be introduced to understand insertion and extraction constraints, station times, reporting procedures, and mobility. For nondivision assets such as theater collection aircraft and national systems, persistence becomes a result of assumptions about time on stations that cover the division's area of interest. In theory, these latter systems could provide constant coverage of at least some of the NAIs, although in practice they doubtless would not.

Responsiveness

The responsiveness factor reflects how long it would take to employ a quick-reaction asset to reconnoiter a particular area. Selection of factor levels for this factor depends on the number and capabilities of the particular scout/recon system assumed dedicated by the division to the responsiveness role. If the same scout/recon resources that are applied to the scheduled missions are also assigned to the quick-reaction force, responsiveness levels must be determined in conjunction with levels of persistence. Other considerations in determining the responsiveness level are the immediate reaction time (time to launch a mission), system speed in moving through the threat environment, and average distance to the area of interest.

Depth and Precision

Mission-dependent factors (vertically slashed boxes in Figure 4.1) are the depth behind the enemy's forward trace that the scout/recon system could penetrate and collect information about the enemy's forces and the precision of the information about the enemy vehicles that it obtains, i.e., detection, classification, or recognition. These factors are determined by simulating scout/recon missions in scenarios developed to represent important operational situations where a heavy division would employ its scout/recon assets. Once the characteristics of the scout/recon system(s) of interest are represented in the simulation environment, the missions are conducted essentially as described in Section 3.

To provide credible mission results, it is important to develop well-designed mission experiments. To the degree possible, designs should adhere to scientific methods such as factorial crossing of multiple operators/pilots with multiple scenarios with multiple scout/recon systems. Items of particular interest should be individually manipulated so as not to confound the results by changing other system features, unless the one is inseparably tied to the other. For example, to investigate options in sensor characteristics, each option should be singularly manipulated without changing other system features such as sensor mounting location, unless a particular sensor option requires a particular mounting location (e.g., radar above the rotor mast) and another sensor option must be mounted elsewhere for technical or other reasons (e.g., impracticality of relocating an existing sensor mounting).

Using the SCRMM

Once all the factor levels have been determined using the above procedures, those levels are provided to the SCRMM, wherein the STFs calculate the MOPs—the percent of NAIs timely covered, the percent of key enemy force elements identified and tracked, and the percent of enemy key force elements defeated. The SCRMM was automated to provide a user-friendly program for assessing the effects of different scout/recon and intelligence system capabilities. The SCRMM program allows a user to easily modify or select factor levels throughout the structure to define systems and conditions of interest and evaluate resulting differences in MOPs. This use of the SCRMM could provide valuable information to development and acquisition decisions beyond that provided for a specific system(s) under consideration.

Analyzing a Specified Scout/Recon System(s)

Evaluating and comparing well-defined scout/recon systems of particular interest are primary purposes of the method and a principal motivation for developing the SCRMM. For each system, the factor levels that uniquely define the system, including the depth and precision factor levels determined by simulations, are input to the SCRMM to compute the MOPs. Systems can be compared directly with analytic measures described above, the MOPs and the readiness substitution measure. The readiness substitution measure is determined either graphically (as shown in Section 5) or by using the SCRMM to compute it by (1) holding all other factor levels constant and (2) sequentially adjusting only the readiness status factor level until the SCRMM computes the same percent of key force elements defeated that was attained by another system to which it is being compared. The difference between the initial readiness status and final readiness status is the readiness substitution comparison measure.

Exploring Notional Systems and Concepts

The SCRMM can be used as a tool to explore the potential values of notional or imprecisely defined scout/recon systems and concepts that can be described by the SCRMM's factors. To assess such systems or concepts, a carefully designed sequence of SCRMM runs would be made that included systematic variation of factor levels spanning the full range of capabilities that might be achieved. If the systems or concepts were sufficiently definable, mission simulations could be conducted to support the SCRMM analyses, perhaps by providing a baseline(s) around which to focus the investigation.

The inverse side of notional systems analysis generates another SCRMM usage that applies to the independent assessment of intelligence collection and situation assessment capabilities to determine factor level requirements or options that would achieve selected MOP values. For example, one might ask what capabilities would be needed to identify 60% of the enemy key force elements. The objective of such an investigation might be to seek the most cost-effective approaches to enhancing intelligence systems to yield desired results. Determining options to achieve selected MOP values would be done by systematically varying one or more factor levels over a sequence of SCRMM runs. Factor level options that emerge from these investigations would suggest where to apply technological or procedural enhancements (e.g., develop fully automated situation assessment processing systems and real-time data inputs).

Sensitivity Analyses

An important application of the SCRMM is to perform sensitivity analyses on the results obtained from analyzing a specified scout/recon system (i.e., how sensitive the MOPs are to changes in the factor levels). In this context, the effect of changing non-mission-dependent factors (e.g., processing, persistence, or responsiveness) can be investigated by simply by changing the relevant factor level(s) and recalculating the analytic measures. However, to investigate sensitivities to changes in scout/recon system characteristics that affect the conduct of the mission may require reconducting the missions. For example, to investigate the effect of increasing the range at which a sensor can detect, classify, or recognize an object, an approximation of the effectiveness change could (depending on the capability of the simulation system) be obtained by changing the sensor characteristics representations in the simulation, replaying (not reconducting) the identical previous missions, and noting the change in precision and depth that could have been achieved with the new sensors. However, to be satisfied with the conclusions, one would have to reconcile them with the consideration that, had the operators had better sensor capability when they conducted the missions, they might have conducted them in a significantly different manner and achieved significantly different results than obtained by simply substituting new sensors into previous missions.

Tradeoff Analyses

Another important application is to identify system enhancements or tradeoffs that yield high marginal payoffs. Identifying tradeoffs and areas of high marginal payoff could follow from a series of properly designed SCRMM computational runs, but it is also a lucrative area to apply graphical analysis.

Numerous tradeoffs among factors can be calculated by the SCRMM program and viewed graphically in the report. An example is provided in Figure 4.2, where the geometric averaging theory's predictions of key enemy force elements identified and tracked are plotted on the y-axis as a function of the percent of NAIs covered by the collection management cell on the x-axis; a separate curve is for each level of information precision—detection, classification, or recognition. The situations shown in Figure 4.2 are as follows: friendlies are in a prepared defense, intelligence information is coming into the situation assessment cell in real time (5 minutes) and is being processed manually. One set of tradeoffs can be viewed from the horizontal line. If information is at the detection level, 70% of the NAIs must be covered by the scout/recon system (x-axis) for the situation assessment cell to be able to identify and track 35% of the key force elements. However, to achieve the same result, only 40% of the NAIs need to be covered if precision is at the classification level and only 25% if precision is at the recognition level.

Hence, enhancing the scout/recon system's sensors could achieve the same situation assessment results as covering more NAIs but with less risk and exposure to the enemy's air defenses.

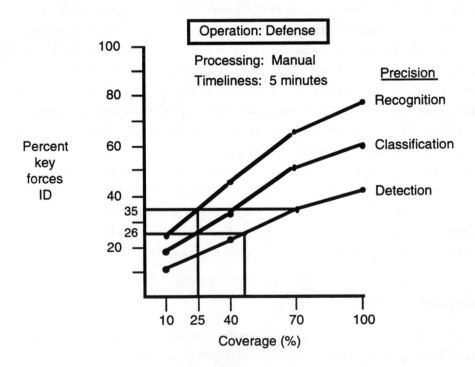

Figure 4.2—Graphical Tradeoff Assessment

Other tradeoffs can be seen in Figure 5.2 and numerous other figures in the report. To direct the reader's attention to the potential tradeoff analyses possible with the graphs presented in the present report, we have constructed some examples using Figures 2.6 to 2.9.

Collection Management. When data are graphed as in Figure 2.6, tradeoffs among the collection management factors in the ability to timely cover NAIs can be seen by imagining or drawing horizontal lines to intersect the curves across panels. For example, compare the squared points in panels D–F of Figure 2.6, where friendlies are in an offensive mode. About 42–47% of the NAIs could be timely covered in all five situations. If intelligence information could be collected only 30 kilometers beyond the enemy's first trace and the Responsiveness capability was as poor as six hours (panel D), Persistence would have to be every 30 minutes (see leftmost square in panel D) to timely cover 44% of the NAIs. However, if collection capability increased to 50 kilometers beyond the enemy's first trace, Persistence could be reduced to one hour (rightmost square in panel D). If Responsiveness could be decreased from six to two hours (panel E), it would be possible to achieve this same percent of essential NAIs covered with a Depth of only 15 kilometers beyond the enemy's first trace if Persistence remained at 30 minutes. However, with a Depth increase to 50 kilometers, Persistence could decrease to three hours. The square shown in panel F shows that with a decrease in Responsiveness to 30 minutes, this same level of effectiveness can be achieved with a Depth of 15 kilometers and a Persistence of one hour.

Numerous tradeoffs like those just described can be seen in these graphs. Because the solid points were constructed from a theory, it is possible to project to physical values other than those actually manipulated in the experiment; that is, all points along the curves can be considered in assessing tradeoffs among the factors in the ability to timely cover NAIs. Such tradeoff analyses could serve as an important input to development and acquisition decisions.

Situation Assessment. In Figures 2.7 and 2.8, interesting tradeoffs among factors can be assessed. For example, identifying and tracking 50% of the key force elements can be accomplished in several ways. When in a defensive mode of operation, if information is at the detection level, it is necessary to cover 100% of the NAIs, get the information to the situation assessment cell in real time, and have at least a semiautomated processing capability (squared point in Figure 2.7D). However, if reported information distinguishes between tracked and wheeled vehicles (i.e., classification) and is reported in real time, processing can be done manually and NAI coverage can drop to 70% (see squared point in Figure 2.7B). If information is at the recognition level with a processing capability remaining at a manual level (Figure 2.7C), it is possible to drop the NAI coverage capability to about 45% if information arrives in real time. The timeliness of information can be as old as 2 hours (120 minutes) for an NAI coverage of 70% when recognition of vehicles is achieved (rightmost square in Figure 2.7C).

Operational Performance. Some interesting operational performance tradeoffs have been delineated with a square in panels E, F, and G of Figure 2.9. The same number of enemy units would be predicted to be defeated from each one of these cases—about 55%. For each case, the division is engaged in a deliberate attack (i.e., is on the offense). If the enemy has been gathering information out to 20 kilometers (i.e., "deep"), the division's readiness status has to be at 95%, and 100% of the key enemy force elements would have to be identified for about 55% of the enemy units to be defeated. When enemy reconnaissance capability reduces to "shallow," the readiness status of the division must be maintained at about 95%, but the key enemy force elements identified can be reduced to about 72%.

In Figure 2.9G, where the enemy's reconnaissance capability has been reduced to observing the division's forward elements only, the division's readiness status can be at 70% if about 77% of the key enemy force elements have been identified by the situation assessment cell; if only 50% have been identified, a readiness status of 95% is necessary. In Figure 2.9H, where the enemy has no reconnaissance capability, 55% of enemy units defeated can be achieved with a readiness status of 70% when only about 62 % of key enemy force elements have been identified. If this identification capability is reduced to around 37%, it is again necessary to have a readiness status of 95% to defeat 55% of the enemy units.

Dealing with Uncertainty

At the beginning of this section we discussed the user's responsibility to design a particular research approach, determine the factor levels for input to the SCRMM, and comprehend and interpret the analytic measures the method produces. How well and carefully this is done will importantly affect the degree of uncertainty that exists in the analytical process, as is the case in any analysis. For example, uncertainties can arise from the fidelity limits of the simulation system in which the scout/recon missions are conducted; or from the confidence in the ability to represent scout/recon system characteristics or, for future systems, to know what they really are; or, for that matter, from the accuracy of any inputs.

With regard to the SCRMM, the measurement theories (STFs) used in the SCRMM are validated representations of the judgment processes of the broadly based groups of SMEs that participated in the model-development experiments; that is, they provide validated predictions of the SMEs' judgments in all situations that can be described by the SCRMM's factors and factor levels. Hence, tradeoff analyses, including the readiness substitution concept, determined using the SCRMM's subjective judgment measurement theories are valid within that context.

A user must also remember that the argument for the SCRMM's results to reflect what would happen in actual combat situations (the "external" validity question) rests in the professional experience and training of the SMEs. The major focus of military training is to achieve a high degree of individual and team proficiency in job performance and to develop a depth of understanding and appreciation for the combat environments in which they must function. Hence, one would expect that the SMEs' judgment predictions with respect to their areas of expertise, while not perfect, provide solid, professional indications of outcomes that could occur in actual situations.

Accommodating to uncertainties should be a major factor in the overall analytic design, influencing the scope of the analysis (number of runs, ranges of factor levels, etc.), the extent of sensitivity analyses, and the interpretation of the results. This is true for any analysis, and the scout/recon analysis method is no different.

5. An Example Application of the Methodology: Comparing Scout/Recon Systems

To bring together the preceding discussions into a more coherent picture, we demonstrate by example how to use the methodology to analyze and compare scout/recon systems that could support heavy division operations. For our example, we choose two types of notional scout/recon systems with very different physical, operational, and technological characteristics to show how disparate systems can produce significantly different *local* results in the model's hierarchical structure and how they can be compared within the operational terms of the model. The systems are notional in the sense that they do not replicate existing or planned systems, even though they characterize existing approaches to providing battlefield intelligence. Hence, it is important for the reader to clearly recognize that our purpose is only to demonstrate the method and the scope of its application.

One type of system (system A) features high-altitude, standoff surveillance with long-range sensors that provide an expansive, low-resolution picture of selected operations areas in the theater, including but not dedicated to the area of interest to a particular heavy division. These assets respond to theater or task force level command and control having responsibilities across the conflict area and scope of air, land, and sea operations. The other type of system (system B) represents advanced scout/recon helicopters assigned to and under direct control of the division. These organic assets operate very near the earth and close to the enemy, and feature short-range sensors technologically capable of providing high-resolution, incremental snapshots within the division's area of interest.

Real application of the methodology is meaningful only within the framework of an analysis designed to achieve some objective that is dependent on or affected by the operational performance of a scout/recon system(s). The analytical framework establishes the issues and alternatives relevant to the objective, and the operational environments and situations and friendly and enemy force postures and capabilities that are essential to the analysis. These provide the basis for designing and constructing the simulation scenarios, designing and conducting the scout/recon missions, and selecting situation assessment support systems and operations alternatives on which to run the model.

Determining Factor Levels

The first step in applying the method is to determine a level for each factor in the STF scout/recon analysis model that describes its state under the specifications of the scenario, the division's posture and assets, and the scout/recon system's characteristics. Since the purpose of applying the method is to analyze selected current or future scout/recon systems under selected operational conditions, the specifications derive from a mix of reality about existing entities, assumptions about unknown or speculative conditions or capabilities, and deliberate selectivity of factor levels to support analytical objectives.

Example Analytical Framework

In our example, we seek to analyze how scout/recon systems A and B could support a heavy division assigned to defend a designated area in terrain typical of much of the northern hemisphere, mildly rolling plains and forested low hills. Our analytical interest focuses on a friendly division in a prepared defense that, because of deployment factors and prior operations, finds the division at 70% readiness. We consider the case where the division's situation assessment cell processes information manually, although it has ready access to display screens integrated with an automatic target handoff system (ATHS) used by its organic artillery observation and advanced scout aircraft such as system B. Further, the division dedicates quick-reaction scout/recon assets that, on average, take about two hours to respond to special intelligence collection requests.

The attacking armor force enjoys a 3:1 force ratio advantage and proceeds to the attack using a road march formation distributed on three parallel avenues of approach spanning 30 kilometers from flank to flank and extending about 100 kilometers from front to rear. In consonance with the model, we are interested in the final 36 hours of operations prior to initial contact in the security zone. These criteria provide the basis for developing the scenarios within which to conduct the simulated scout/recon missions.

As an initial condition for the example analysis, we assume that the division's counterreconnaissance capability can limit the enemy's reconnaissance units to making contact only with the covering force, i.e., the *forward force elements*.[1]

---

[1]The example analytical framework has been seriously abbreviated for our demonstration purposes. Typically, it would include several factor sets or ranges, specific operational or conditional excursions, and sensitivity analyses.

Scout/Recon System Characteristics and Mission-Dependent Factors

The analytical framework includes defining the characteristics of the scout/recon systems that are relevant to the analysis. Given the general descriptions above, two system-dependent factors remain, persistence and timeliness. The issues that drive how often scout/recon systems A and B could reconnoiter the NAIs differ entirely for the two systems. System A's availability to the division area is controlled at theater level and depends on alternative requirements and priorities pertaining to activities throughout the theater as well as on the number of A-type aircraft assigned to the theater. For purposes of the example, we will assume that system A would be made available to provide surveillance of the division's area every three hours. System A reports the objects it senses to an associated ground facility for processing and distribution to the division through a theater intelligence network. We further assume that the information arrives at the division situation assessment cell three hours after system A collects it.[2]

System B's availability depends on the number of B-type helicopters assigned to the division, their maintainability, and the division's decision to commit them to reconnoitering the enemy's advance. Current Army force modernization plans include sufficient numbers of advanced scout aircraft in the heavy division to support a scout/recon mission every three hours throughout the 36-hour period based on calculations similar to those shown in Section 3. Using the ATHS capability discussed above, system B can provide collected data to the situation assessment cell in near real time, say within five minutes of an observation.

Hence, under the assumptions of the example, the persistence factor level is three hours for both systems and the timeliness factor level is two hours for system A and five minutes for system B.

The precision of the information (i.e., detection, classification, or recognition) reported to division intelligence stems from a combination of the system's technological characteristics and its operational tactics and procedures. For system A, we ascribe to it a technology that can provide detection of objects across the full range of its sensor, but cannot classify or recognize them, at least not at the farther reaches of its capability. System A survives by operating over friendly controlled or otherwise safe territory and maintaining a standoff distance beyond the range

---

[2]Clearly other assumptions could be entertained both with regard to the frequency with which a theater asset would reconnoiter a division's area of interest and how the information could be provided to the division, such as direct readout at the division; however, we consider these assumptions to fall within the general range of conditions that would exist in future conflicts involving heavy division operations.

of enemy air defense systems. Considering those two factors and the geographical movement of the enemy forces over the course of a 36-hour road march, we estimate that system A could provide detection data to an average depth of 75 kilometers behind the enemy's forward trace over the 36-hour period of interest.

The precision of the information collected by system B results from the confluence of its sensor technology, its ability to physically position itself to bring the sensors to bear, and its survivability. These elements are interdependent. The sensor range affects the latitude for maneuver to find objects and avoid air defenses. Aircraft survival characteristics (e.g., signatures) affect how close the aircraft can be safely positioned to enemy forces, increasing the opportunity for greater precision observations by its sensor. There is also interaction between precision and depth of NAI coverage because the more difficult it is to find and develop sensed objects, the more time and fuel is consumed, lessening how deeply the aircraft can penetrate before it reaches its endurance limits. In actual application of the methodology, the complex effects of these interdependencies is resolved by representing the scout/recon system characteristics in a simulation model and conducting a well-designed set of scout/recon missions as described in Section 4. Drawing on the preliminary missions flown during the development of the methodology, for the example we will estimate that a system B mission will penetrate 40 kilometers behind the enemy forward trace when it operates so as to recognize the enemy weapon systems moving in the vicinity of the assigned NAIs.

Factor Levels for the Example

The above discussions provide sufficient information to establish a level for both the situation assessment and the operations measurement model. Table 5.1 summarizes the scout/recon system-independent factor levels that result from the example analytical framework.

Table 5.1

System-Independent Factor Levels

Operation	Defense
Readiness status	70%
Enemy scout/recon performance	Contact with forward force elements only
Processing	Manual
Responsiveness	2 hours

Table 5.2 summarizes the scout/recon system- and mission-dependent factors.

Table 5.2

Scout/Recon System- and Mission-Dependent Factor Levels

Factor	System A	System B
Persistence	3 hours	3 hours
Timeliness	2 hours	5 minutes
Precision	Detection	Recognition
Depth	75 kilometers	40 kilometers

Calculating and Comparing the Value of Systems A and B

Once the factor levels are determined that represent a particular analytical situation, they are input to the SCRMM's program that calculates the factors Coverage, Key Force Elements Identified, and Enemy Units Defeated. Alternatively, a graphical analysis can be done that presents a good visual representation of how the factors affect the results. For the reader's benefit, we will use the graphical approach, depicting system A with a square symbol and system B with a round symbol; all graphs pertain to the division in a *defense* operation.

The graphs in the right panel of Figure 5.1 show the percent of NAIs that could be timely covered if the quick-reaction force could respond to special requests in two hours. System A's 75-kilometer depth of coverage and 3-hour persistence results in timely coverage of 40% of the essential NAIs. System B's 40-kilometer depth of coverage and 3-hour persistence results in timely coverage of 30% of the essential NAIs. Hence, system A covers a third more NAIs than does system B.

In the left panel of Figure 5.1, the graphs show the percent of key force elements that could be identified using manual situation assessment processing. The lower line reflects a *detection* precision level coupled with a 2-hour timeliness level; the upper line reflects a *recognition* precision level coupled with a 5-minute timeliness level. For system A we enter the chart at the 40% coverage determined on the right panel and, using the lower line, determine that with system A providing the scout/recon inputs, 14% of the key enemy force elements could be identified and tracked. Entering the chart at the 30% coverage point that system B could achieve, we see that because of system B's higher precision and near-real-time data input, 37% of the key enemy force elements could be identified and tracked. Note that the importance attributed by situation assessment officers to recognition over detection is so great that even if system A had been able to cover

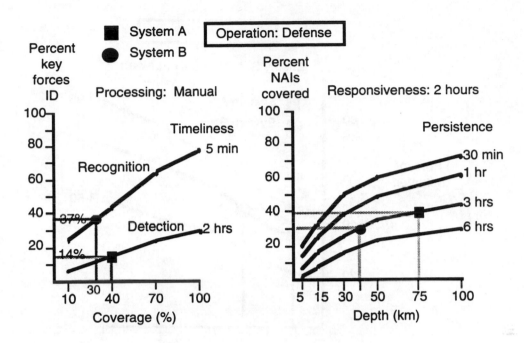

Figure 5.1—Graphical Assessment of Dissimilar Scout/Recon Assets: Coverage and Key Elements Identified

all of the NAIs, its contribution to enemy force element identification (just under 30%) would still have fallen well short of system B's contribution.

Figure 5.2 shows the percent of key enemy force elements that the division could defeat when the enemy's scout/recon forces could only observe the forwardmost friendly forces (the covering force). Each line in the graph represents outcomes for a different division operational readiness level.

For the selected readiness of 70%, first observe that if the situation assessment capability is unable to identify any of the enemy's forces, the division could defeat slightly more than 30% of the key enemy force elements. Given the 14% identification level resulting from system A's inputs, the division could defeat 35% of the enemy key force elements; with system B, 46% could be defeated.

Hence, the SCRMM results indicate that

- System A's inputs result in division operational effectiveness (measured by enemy units defeated) slightly better (by one-sixth) than having no scout/recon inputs.

- System B's inputs result in division operational effectiveness approximately one-third greater than if system A provided the scout/recon support and over one-half greater than having no inputs.

54

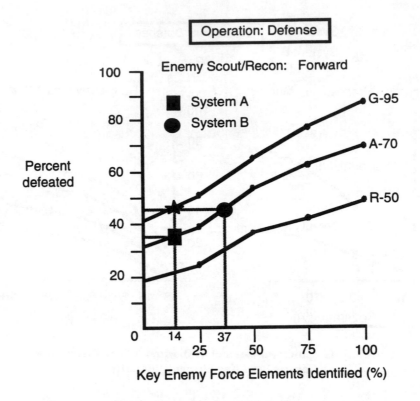

Figure 5.2—Graphical Assessment of Dissimilar Scout/Recon Assets: Enemy Force Elements Defeated

Another perspective on these results comes from the "readiness substitution" concept described in Section 4 that interprets the difference in operations performance in terms of the difference in division readiness needed to achieve the same performance level. In our example, we can determine from Figure 5.2 the increase from 70% readiness that produces the same percent defeated with system A that was produced by system B (46%). Regardless of readiness level, with system A, 14% of key enemy force elements are identified. From Figure 5.2 we see that in order to defeat 46% of the enemy force elements when only 14% of them are identified, operational readiness would need to be increased from 70% to 94%.

Hence, under the conditions of the example, we would conclude that the difference in a heavy division's operational effectiveness with system B compared to system A is the same as a 24% increase in the division's readiness—roughly equivalent to the division having one additional operationally ready armor brigade.

6. Summary Remarks

We have developed a method to measure the value of scout/recon in support of heavy division operations. It features the application of modern subjective measurement to develop a model, the SCRMM, of the human processes—the division intelligence staff's performance of collection management and situation assessment, and the contribution of these activities to the division's operational performance. The method also incorporates the simulation of scout/recon system missions in high-resolution combat models to provide inputs to the SCRMM. We believe the approach yields credible analytic results and can provide a reasonable basis to inform system development and acquisition as well as doctrinal decisions under uncertainty.

To demonstrate the methodology, we constructed an example with two hypothetical but technologically feasible systems and showed how the method can be used to determine the value of each system with regard to its contribution to division operational effectiveness. In addition to directly comparing their values, we compared them by equating their difference in value to differences in division readiness, which equates roughly to additional forces that would be required to achieve the better result—a direct connection to the force multiplier concept.

The reader is reminded that the situation assessment and operations model applies only to heavy divisions, having been developed from the judgments of intelligence and operations officers about heavy divisions imminently to be engaged in combat with large, modern, enemy armored forces. It does not apply to light force operations or operations other than war.

To measure the value of scout/recon in support of light force operations, the same general approach would pertain. For light forces, however, the analysis would address different combat situations, most likely requiring different MOPs that depend on somewhat different processes. This would require developing appropriate operating concepts and the situation assessment and operations models that reflect those concepts in terms of both processes and MOPs. One would also need to develop and operationalize combat scenarios relevant to future worldwide light force projections and expand the military context for scout/recon to include low-intensity conflicts featuring prolonged maneuvering preceding selected combat that could include highly mobile small-unit strikes, indirect fire, and combat with less-than-leading-edge enemy forces in moderate-size battles.

Appendix

A. Experimental Designs for Judgment Experiments

Collection Management

For the Collection Management Questionnaire, 120 situations were generated by manipulating the factors shown in Figure 2.2 in full factorial designs where every factor level was combined with every other factor level: each of the five Depth factor levels was combined with each of the four Persistence, three Responsiveness, and two Operation levels; each situation consisted of four pieces of information. In addition, subsets of the complete design containing three, two, and one piece(s) of information were included in the questionnaire for purposes of testing among some algebraic measurement theories otherwise incapable of distinction. These designs were constructed as follows:

- Three-way factorial designs
  - Operation × Responsiveness × Persistence (2 × 3 × 4)
  - Operation × Depth × Responsiveness (2 × 5 × 3)
  - Operation × Depth × Persistence (2 × 5 × 4)

These three designs produced 94 situations described by three pieces of information.

- Two-way factorial designs
  - Responsiveness × Persistence (3 × 4)
  - Operation × Depth (2 × 5)
  - Responsiveness × Depth (3 × 5)
  - Operation × Responsiveness (2 × 3)
  - Operation × Persistence (2 × 4)

These five designs produced 51 situations described by two pieces of information.

- One-way designs
  - Operation (2)
  - Persistence (4)
  - Responsiveness (3)
  - Depth (5)

These four designs produced 14 situations described by one piece of information.

For each of the 279 situations produced by this design, which varied the amount of information presented to respondents for judgment, collection management officers judged the percent of essential NAIs that could be timely covered.

Situation Assessment

The experimental design for the Situation Assessment Questionnaire followed the same idea as that described above for the collection management experiment. Since five factors were included in this design (see Figure 2.4), the questionnaire was longer.

The complete factorial design was a $5 \times 4 \times 3 \times 3 \times 2$ (Coverage $\times$ Timeliness $\times$ Precision $\times$ Processing $\times$ Operation) design that produced 360 situations of five pieces of information each. The subdesigns were as follows:

- Three-way factorial designs
  - Operation $\times$ Coverage $\times$ Precision ($2 \times 4 \times 3$)
  - Operation $\times$ Timeliness $\times$ Coverage ($2 \times 4 \times 4$)

These two designs produced 56 situations with three pieces of information in each situation.

- 2-way factorial designs
  - Operation $\times$ Coverage (2×4)
  - Precision $\times$ Processing (3×3)
  - Operation $\times$ Timeliness (2×4)
  - Timeliness $\times$ Precision (4×3)
  - Operation $\times$ Processing (2×3)
  - Coverage $\times$ Processing (4×3)

These six designs produced 61 situations with two pieces of information per situation.

- One-way designs
  - Timeliness (4)
  - Precision (3)
  - Operation (2)
  - Coverage (4)
  - Processing (3)

These five designs produced 21 situations, each containing one piece of information.

For each of the 544 situations described above, situation assessment officers judged the percent of enemy key force elements that could be identified and tracked.

Operational Performance

The Operational Performance Questionnaire contained a total of 260 experimental situations generated using the same kind of varying-sized factorial designs as for the collection management and situation awareness experiments. The fully crossed design generated 120 situations (factors and factor levels are shown in Figure 2.5). The subdesigns were as follows:

- Three-way factorial designs
  — Operation × Key Enemy Force Elements Identified × Readiness Status $(2 \times 5 \times 4)$
  — Operation × Enemy Scout/Recon Performance × Readiness Status $(2 \times 4 \times 4)$
  — Operation × Enemy Scout/Recon Performance × Key Enemy Force Elements Identified $(2 \times 4 \times 5)$

These three designs produced 112 situations containing three pieces of information.

- Two-way factorial designs
  — Operation × Enemy Scout/Recon Performance (2×4)
  — Operation × Key Enemy Force Elements Identified (2×5)
  — Operation × Readiness Status (2×4)

These three designs produced 26 situations, each described by two pieces of information.

- One-way design
  — Operation (2)

This single design produced two situations containing one piece of information.

For each of the 260 situations generated from these designs, operations officers judged the number of key enemy force elements that could be defeated.

B. Situation Assessment Questionnaire

On the following pages is the questionnaire used to judge the "percent of key enemy force elements that could be identified and tracked." The matrices that form the questionnaire reflect the experimental design for the situation assessment judgment tasks described in Appendix A.

% of key enemy force elements that could be identified and tracked

OPERATION: DEFENSE

PRECISION: DETECTION

	Timeliness	Coverage				
		0%	10%	40%	70%	100%
Processing: Manual	6 hrs					
	2 hrs					
	45 min					
	5 min					
Processing: Semi- Automated	6 hrs					
	2 hrs					
	45 min					
	5 min					
Processing: Fully- Automated	6 hrs					
	2 hrs					
	45 min					
	5 min					

% of key enemy force elements that could be identified and tracked

OPERATION: DEFENSE

PRECISION: CLASSIFICATION

	Timeliness	Coverage				
		0%	10%	40%	70%	100%
Processing: Manual	6 hrs					
	2 hrs					
	45 min					
	5 min					
Processing: Semi-Automated	6 hrs					
	2 hrs					
	45 min					
	5 min					
Processing: Fully-Automated	6 hrs					
	2 hrs					
	45 min					
	5 min					

% of key enemy force elements that could be identified and tracked

OPERATION: DEFENSE

PRECISION: RECOGNITION

	Timeliness	Coverage				
		0%	10%	40%	70%	100%
Processing: Manual	6 hrs					
	2 hrs					
	45 min					
	5 min					
Processing: Semi-Automated	6 hrs					
	2 hrs					
	45 min					
	5 min					
Processing: Fully-Automated	6 hrs					
	2 hrs					
	45 min					
	5 min					

% of key enemy force elements that could be identified and tracked

OPERATION: OFFENSE

PRECISION: DETECTION

	Timeliness	Coverage				
		0%	10%	40%	70%	100%
Processing: Manual	6 hrs					
	2 hrs					
	45 min					
	5 min					
Processing: Semi-Automated	6 hrs					
	2 hrs					
	45 min					
	5 min					
Processing: Fully-Automated	6 hrs					
	2 hrs					
	45 min					
	5 min					

% of key enemy force elements that could be identified and tracked

OPERATION: OFFENSE

PRECISION: CLASSIFICATION

		Coverage				
	Timeliness	0%	10%	40%	70%	100%
Processing: Manual	6 hrs					
	2 hrs					
	45 min					
	5 min					
Processing: Semi-Automated	6 hrs					
	2 hrs					
	45 min					
	5 min					
Processing: Fully-Automated	0 hrs					
	2 hrs					
	45 min					
	5 min					

% of key enemy force elements that could be identified and tracked

OPERATION: OFFENSE

PRECISION: RECOGNITION

	Timeliness	Coverage				
		0%	10%	40%	70%	100%
Processing: Manual	6 hrs					
	2 hrs					
	45 min					
	5 min					
Processing: Semi-Automated	6 hrs					
	2 hrs					
	45 min					
	5 min					
Processing: Fully-Automated	6 hrs					
	2 hrs					
	45 min					
	5 min					

% of key enemy force elements that could be identified and tracked

OPERATION: OFFENSE

PRECISION: RECOGNITION

	Timeliness	Coverage				
		0%	10%	40%	70%	100%
Processing: Manual	6 hrs					
	2 hrs					
	45 min					
	5 min					
Processing: Semi-Automated	6 hrs					
	2 hrs					
	45 min					
	5 min					
Processing: Fully-Automated	6 hrs					
	2 hrs					
	45 min					
	5 min					

% of key enemy force elements that could be identified and tracked

Operation	Timeliness			
	6 hrs	2 hrs	45 min	5 min
Defense				
Offense				

Timeliness	Precision		
	Detect	Classify	Recognize
6 hrs			
2 hrs			
45 min			
5 min			

Operation	Processing		
	Manual	Semi-Automated	Fully Automated
Defense			
Offense			

% of key enemy force elements that could be identified and tracked

Timeliness			
6 hrs	2 hrs	45 min	5 min

	Timeliness	Coverage				
		0%	10%	40%	70%	100%
D e f e n s e	6 hrs					
	2 hrs					
	45 min					
	5 min					
O f f e n s e	6 hrs					
	2 hrs					
	45 min					
	5 min					

Precision		
Detection	Classification	Recognition

% of key enemy force elements that could identified and tracked

Operation	Precision		
	Detect	Classify	Recognize
Defense			
Offense			

Operation	
Defense	Offense

Coverage				
0%	10%	40%	70%	100%

Coverage	Processing		
	Manual	Semi Automated	Fully Automated
0%			
10%			
40%			
70%			
100%			

Processing		
Manual	Semi-Automated	Fully Automated

C. The RAND Combat Analysis Environment (CAE)

RAND has a suite of high-resolution, interfaced models in its Combat Analysis Environment (CAE) that provide the capability to operate scout/recon systems against representative ground force laydowns. Figure C.1 depicts the models and interconnections in the CAE. Although the CAE includes an open-architecture version of JANUS, only the higher-resolution elements that are shaded on the chart would be used for these missions.

CAGIS (Zobrist, Marcelino, and Daniels, 1991) is a micro-terrain model that represents foliage and cultural features as well as earth contours. Conflict scenarios are represented on the CAGIS fixed database by initial placement of weapon system icons and specification of the systems' static, dynamic, and operational characteristics. CAGIS includes a mission profile generator, which is used interactively by an operator to "fly" or "drive" a mission from a workstation using the helicopter flight planner (HFP), the fixed-wing aircraft flight planner (FWFP), or the ground vehicle route planner (GVRP). The operator interacts with a graphic (plan view/overhead or out-the-window) display, on a multicolor monitor, of the terrain and weapon systems that are within his line of sight. The operator also receives indications of threats, such as air defense radar signals, on his survival equipment displays. Only information that an operator would have available based on his own system's position and sensor characteristics and the relative positions, signatures, and emissions of other systems at any moment in time is presented, and then only to the degree of precision (detection, classification, recognition, identification) allowed by the capability of his eyes or sensors. If the operator's simulated weapon system has a means to store observed data for later consideration (e.g., the positions of threat radars or detected vehicles), then the operator can activate this capability and review previous inputs or observations. Based on this dynamic information and the tactics and doctrine appropriate to the mission, operators incrementally select three-dimensional points through which they desire to pass and thereby incrementally determine an entire mission profile.

CHAMP (LaForge, Jennings, and Zobrist, 1990) is the helicopter flight dynamics program that determines the actual helicopter flight profile that would result from the step-by-step path called for by a pilot and constrains the pilot to feasible flight maneuvers. For example, a pilot cannot turn tighter or climb faster or

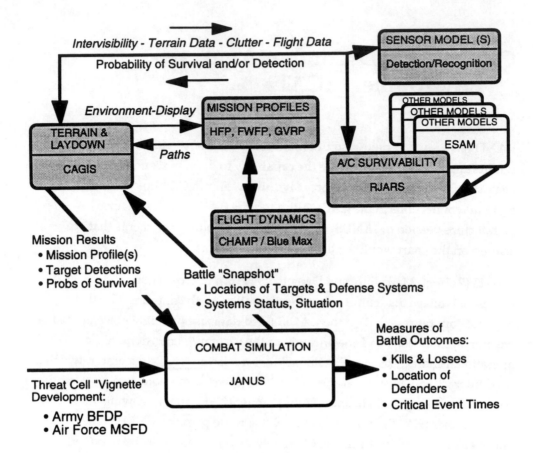

Figure C.1—Combat Analysis Environment (CAE)

higher than the performance characteristics of the simulated aircraft would allow. Currently CHAMP contains the flight dynamics data for a number of Army aircraft, including the RAH-66, AH-64, OH-58D, an unmanned aerial vehicle, and a tactical tilt rotor.

RJARS (Sollfrey, 1991, 1992) is a high-resolution air defense model. Once a flight profile is generated, CAGIS simulates the mission and determines the line-of-sight (LOS) exposure windows between the aircraft and the air defense weapon systems included in the scenario. RJARS processes the LOS windows between the aircraft and the air defense units, determines if the aircraft was detected, tracked, and engaged, and calculates the probability of survival for each engagement and the cumulative probability over all engagements. RJARS integrates the aircraft's radar and infrared signature data for the entire sphere surrounding the aircraft (based on horizontal and vertical signature data provided for each aircraft), accounts for radar and infrared clutter and radar jamming, and determines air defense system effectiveness based on the precise aircraft aspect exposed to the air defense sensors.

References

Anderson, N. H., "Functional Measurement and Psychophysical Judgment," *Psychological Review*, Vol. 77, 1970, pp. 153–170.

Anderson, N. H., *Foundations of Information Integration Theory*, New York: Academic Press, 1981.

Birnbaum, M. H., "The Nonadditivity of Personality Impressions," *Journal of Experimental Psychology Monograph*, Vol. 67, 1974, pp. 555–563.

Birnbaum, M. H., "Difference and Ratios in Psychological Measurement," in N. J. Castellan and F. Restle (eds.), *Cognitive Theory*, vol. 3, Hillsdale, N. J.: Lawrence Erlbaum Associates, 1978, pp. 33–74.

Birnbaum, M. H., "Comparison of Two Theories of 'Ratio' and 'Difference' Judgments," *Journal of Experimental Psychology: General*, Vol. 109, 1980, pp. 304–319.

Birnbaum, M. H., "On Rescaling Data to Fit the Model and Concluding That the Model Fits: A Note on Monotonic Transformation," *Perception and Psychophysics*, Vol. 32, 1982, pp. 293–296.

Birnbaum, M. H., G. Coffey, B. A. Mellers, and R. Weiss, "Utility Measurement: Configural-Weight Theory and the Judge's Point of View," *Journal of Experimental Psychology: Human Perception and Performance*, Vol. 18, No. 2, 1992, pp. 331–346.

Birnbaum, M. H., A. Parducci, and R. K. Gifford, "Contextual Effects in Information Integration," *Journal of Experimental Psychology*, Vol. 88, No. 2, 1971, pp. 158–170.

Birnbaum, M. H., and Y. Sotoodeh, "Measurement of Stress: Scaling the Magnitudes of Life Changes," *Psychological Science*, Vol. 2, 1991, pp. 236–243.

Birnbaum, M. H., and C. T. Veit, "Scale-Free Tests of an Averaging Model for the Size-Weight Illusion," *Perception and Psychophysics*, Vol. 16, 1974a, pp. 276–282.

Birnbaum, M. H., and C. T. Veit, "Scale Convergence as a Criterion for Rescaling: Information Integration with Difference, Ratio, and Averaging Tasks," *Perception and Psychophysics*, Vol. 15, 1974b, pp. 7–15.

Klinger, J. S., *Analysts Manual for Bluemax-II, Version 1.2*, Department of Operations Research, Fairchild/Republic Company.

Krantz, D. H., R. D. Luce, P. Suppes, and A. Tversky, *Foundations of Measurement*, vol. 1, New York: Academic Press, 1971.

Krantz, D. H., and A. Tversky, "Conjoint-Measurement Analysis of Composition Rules in Psychology," *Psychological Review*, Vol. 78, 1971, pp. 151–169.

LaForge, S., J. Jennings, and A. L. Zobrist, "CHAMP: A Helicopter/VTOL Flight Model for Integrated Operational Analysis," *Proceedings of the American Helicopter Society*, Washington, D.C., 1990.

Mellers, B., "Equity Judgment: A Revision of Aristotelian Views," *Journal of Experimental Psychology: General*, Vol. 111, No. 2, 1982, pp. 242–270.

Mellers, B. A., D. Davis, and M. H. Birnbaum, "Weight of Evidence Supports One Operation for 'Ratios' and 'Differences' of Heaviness," *Journal of Experimental Psychology: Human Perception and Performance*, Vol. 10, 1984, pp. 216–230.

Sollfrey, W., *RJARS: RAND's Version of the Jamming Aircraft and Radar Simulation*, Santa Monica, CA: RAND, N-2727-1-AF/A/DARPA/DR&E, 1991.

Sollfrey, W., *RJARS: RAND's Version of the Jamming Aircraft and Radar Simulation, Developments in 1991*, Santa Monica, CA: RAND, N-2727-1/1-AF/PA&E/OSD, 1992.

Veit, C. T., "Ratio and Subtractive Processes in Psychophysical Judgment," *Journal of Experimental Psychology: General*, Vol. 107, No. 1, 1978, pp. 81–107.

Veit, C. T., and M. Callero, *Subjective Transfer Function Approach to Complex System Analysis*, Santa Monica, CA: RAND, R-2719-AF, 1981.

Veit, C. T., M. Callero, and B. J. Rose, *Demonstration of the Subjective Transfer Function Approach Applied to Air-Force-Wide Mission Area Analysis*, Santa Monica, CA: RAND, N-1831-AF, 1982.

Veit, C. T., M. Callero, and B. J. Rose, *Introduction to the Subjective Transfer Function Approach to Analyzing Systems*, Santa Monica, CA: RAND, R-3021-AF, 1984.

Veit, C. T., B. J. Rose, and M. Callero, *Subjective Measurement of Tactical Air Command and Control—Vol. III: Investigation of Enemy Information Components*, Santa Monica, CA: RAND, N-1671/3-AF, 1980.

Veit, C. T., B. J. Rose, and J. E. Ware, "Effects of Physical and Mental Health on Health-State Preferences," *Medical Care*, Vol. 20, No. 4, 1982, pp. 386–401.

Weber, E. U., C. J. Anderson, and M. H. Birnbaum, "A Theory of Perceived Risk and Attractiveness," *Journal of Organizational Behavior and Human Decision Processes*, Vol. 51, 1992, pp. 492–523.

Zobrist, A. L., L. J. Marcelino, and G. S. Daniels, *RAND's Cartographic Analysis and Geographic Information System (RAND-CAGIS): A Guide to System Use*, Santa Monica, CA: RAND, N-3172-RC, 1991.